Her Redemption Song

Her Salvaged Chariot, Crouching Tiger, Hidden Lamb

"A book is less important for What it says than for what it makes you think!"

~Louis L'Amour

TINA AMELIA WEDDLE

Copyright © 2024
All Rights Reserved
ISBN:

Disclaimer: The names of the people represented in this book have been changed to protect their privacy.

Dedication

I'd like to dedicate this Book to every person I have ever known. Each and every person who has crossed my path in this life and who has yet to cross my path has been preordained to either be a blessing or a lesson. I welcome You to be of good courage because We each have something in common. We come into this world without instruction, each attempting to find our way. We either become our own best friend or our own worst enemy. In time, we may each learn to make peace with the simple truth that as we invest in our true destiny, which is eternity, we will either be someone's blessing or their worst memory. May we strive to be that person who leaves people with good memories when they think about us, for they will never forget how we made them feel. Make this life your fingerprint for the good. You don't have to be rich or poor to make a difference, even if that difference is solely for Ourselves. May we continue to raise the vibration of this earth for the positive as we continue to evolve.

Acknowledgment

I acknowledge the people, my publicist, and the Editing team who helped me put my book together into a format that expresses my true essence as I attempt to put my experiences down into words. It could never replace real-time, but it comes close. I cried many tears expressing my life experiences and recalling the people and events I encountered along the way. I am grateful to each of you for helping me put my thoughts into words. Thank you!

CONTENTS

Dedication iii

Acknowledgment iv

About the Author vi

Preface vii

Chapter 1 STEPPING OUT OF THE DARK 1

Chapter 2 INTO THE LIGHT, BACK TO LIFE, BACK TO REALITY
.... 14

Chapter 3 OPEN THE EYES TO MY HEART 30

Chapter 4 A VISITING ANGEL ENCOUNTER 42

Chapter 5 EXPERIENCING MIRACLES, SIGNS, AND WONDERS
.... 53

Chapter 6 COVID 19 HITS HARD 58

Chapter 7 THE IMPORTANCE OF MENTORS 69

Chapter 8 SPIRITUALITY & SPIRITUAL THINGS 79

Chapter 9 SEARCHING FOR TRUTHS 90

Chapter 10 ADVENTURES AND MEMORIALS BEYOND THE VEIL
.... 105

Chapter 11 I'M GOING HOME 124

Chapter 12 MUSIC; THIS IS MY SONG 131

Chapter 13 THE ART & BEAUTY OF SURRENDER 138

Chapter 14 FINDING OZ 145

About the Author

Tina Amelia Weddle is the author of two Books in a series: the first, "Crouching Tiger, Hidden Lamb, & Her Salvaged Chariot," and the second, *"Her Redemption Song."*

Tina resides in California and is a registered nurse with 30 years of experience in the medical field. Through her life experiences & her strong faith in God, Tina has chosen to believe in miracles & the art of *Hope*. Nothing happens by chance & as long as we are willing, we can turn our lives around and turn them into our own personal redemption song.

Preface

I arise in the silence of dawn
Just at the break of the day

Withdrawn to a desolate place
I bow down to pray.

This place is well-known to merchants,
shepherds, thieves, and saints

Each seeking, each longing for change
Recompense for a better way

My soul rests here.

In silent surrender

In lieu of my will
For his saving grace

All my wealth I've given to strangers
Wandered the desert so wearily

Left weeping, beaten, defeated, void
Lest I embrace thee- sour adversity.

A Barren Vessel I've poured out.
Tears of stone from Clay

Now Seeking Refuge
On this Holy ground, I do declare

Abased in recognition of my state
Robed in my despair

On bleeding Knees
I vow to plead
My head hung low
In shame & defeat

A Sacrificial Prayer of Surrender

Humbled Prostate
I cast my Crown at your feet

Before this long day wanes
And My lowly body grows Weak.

All IN All, He presumed my fall
though I Have nothing to offer A king

My only Hope
*Here in the love of Christ; Tis Not too late to Seek

Chapter 1

STEPPING OUT OF THE DARK

Why is it that some people are more inclined to place themselves in harm's way to help and save others yet less inclined to risk the same to save themselves?

I would manage to escape a torturous and abusive situation, but now I had to face a hard reality.

I am now 19 years old and a single mom. I find myself in an awful dilemma as a high school dropout, currently homeless, and lacking any job skills. Intensifying my troubles, I am desperately fleeing from a deranged partner who harbors an evil desire to see me dead rather than allow me to escape alive.

Fearful and painfully shy, I was in a perpetual state of awkwardness. The five years of isolation I endured made me cautious to the highest degree whenever I found myself in public spaces or around people in general.

I realized that I could not manage to move forward if I continued doing this, so I knew I had to pull myself up by my bootstraps!

I started checking off my list:

1. Enroll in college.
2. Purchase reliable transportation.
3. Get a job.
4. Get my Diploma.
5. Decide what I will do with my future.

Next, I need to heal!!

I joined my mom's church in downtown Sacramento and was welcomed into the family with open arms.

Stepping back into society was not an easy task after enduring years of isolation as I grappled with the lingering effects it had left behind. I had to deal with the feelings of insecurity and inadequacy.

I was determined to get back to whatever "Normal" was, and I had to start somewhere. Lifting my head up and looking people in the face and into their eyes when spoken to was an awkward struggle, and I felt like a scared little mouse, vulnerable and easily startled.

I went up for Altar Call every single Sunday, surrendering on bent knees and begging God for help to heal me and to make me "Normal." I asked God to relieve me of my fears.

Stepping out in boldness and faith, I joined Youth Ministries and signed up to teach Sunday School. I passed out church tracks and put my best foot forward in order to initiate conversations. It was frightening; I stuttered; I flinched at sudden movements, expecting to get smacked for saying the wrong thing. I was extremely sensitive, and I cried easily. I was truly "A Mess."

I decided to take self-defense classes and self-help studies and signed up for counseling. I prayed often, asked God for deliverance, and read every book of encouragement that I could possibly get my hands on!

Then, I started a journal, and I tried to put The Last Five Years completely behind me.

I purchased my first vehicle—a huge, maroon Buick owned by an elderly gentleman who took great care of it. It was immaculate, and the back seat perfectly accommodated my children's car seats.

Our Pastor offered me a job with his friends in a Cafe in Downtown Sacramento Serving STATE workers. I admired the confidence and demeanor of the clientele I served, and I vowed to be just as confident in the candor of their speech one day soon.

I eventually saved up enough money to move out on my own. I obtained my High School degree and enrolled in SAC City College. The feeling I had when I walked onto the College grounds was like Rocky Balboa stepping into the boxing ring with the confidence of the winner!

As I passed by the crowd, I whispered, "Thank you very much," and nodded in approval as if the crowd was cheering me on. Deep down, I knew this was not the case, but one could indulge in daydreams.

I familiarized myself with the Bus System and took the City Buses to commute to school, a self-made choice to save the hard-earned money from working at the Cafe. Gradually, my life was slowly coming together, and I owed God all the glory.

I often thought about my family and the sense of freedom I felt while growing up with such unity and love. Before going forward, I'm flooded with so many valuable memories from my upbringing as the youngest among seven children. It brings to mind the fact that my mother, a middle child, was raised along with 16 living siblings. Plus, my father's large family was rooted in West Sacramento.

When I was born without a dad of my own, he took me in his arms, named me after his own mother, and adopted me as his child. One of my favorite trips to my Dad's Mom's house (Paternal Grandmother) was the downtown bridge that parted in two to allow the large boats to pass through.

Upon crossing into West SAC, my dad would make a stop at a small gas station on the roadside. The bell would ring, and a friendly service attendant would come out to pump gas for us. Once the task was completed, he'd pull out a long string of multi-colored lollipops for us kids to enjoy. Dad would graciously give the man a modest tip, and this became a delightful routine in our journeys.

While traveling along the road to West SAC, near the sand dunes of The Discovery Park River, my mom allowed us kids the freedom to play during the summertime. In that area, there Stood an old, abandoned cement building that we'd deemed as "Haunted." It stood tall and grim with open windows, shrouded in darkness, resembling an abandoned Castle. From the road, those windows appeared pitch black, and we often spotted bats that circled the building.

Sitting huddled with my siblings in the back seat of our old Chevy, my imagination ran wild. I conjured images of ghostly apparitions swirling through the air, poised to seize any unsuspecting soul daring enough to venture into their haunted realm, much like the eerie tale depicted in the song "Hotel California." We held an unwavering belief that once someone stepped foot inside, they would be forever trapped, never to check out.

I'm reminded of a time when we were younger, way before Mom was committed to serving God. She'd decided to have some fun with us kids and rounded us up to have a Seance in our backyard.

We waited for the sun to go down, and Mom sat each of us, Indian-style, side by side in a circle. Holding hands, with Mom as the Leader. Mom placed a candle in the center of the circle, and she took the lead of the ring. Once everyone was still and quiet, Mom began to chant, "Bloody Mary, Bloody Mary. If you can hear us, make a train go by." Right as she said that last word, a train came swiftly and loudly, rushing past!

Never mind the fact that we lived right next to a railroad track. We all screamed, terrified, jumped up, and scattered! Our little legs scrambled as fast as we could for safety towards the back door of our house, shoving each other out of the way, leaving panting!

We were scared witless. Not one of us ever agreed to a seance again!

My Uncle Jazz was one of the first people we ever knew who had a television in his car! He rolled up to our house in his shiny Cadillac and piled all of us— Mom and Dad and us kids, into his car. He took us up to pick blackberries, and I ended up getting my fingers slammed into his car door. I still suffer from nerve pain in my fingers when it gets cold outdoors to remind me of that special day. I will always remember that shiny Cadillac with a TV in the back.

Another Uncle, Job, was a very cool guy. He always wore a coin in his ear in case he needed to make a phone call, slicked-back hair, leather gloves with cut-off fingers, and a car with an "Ooga Ooga horn." He was a riot and got quite rowdy at Dominoes and sports bets; he was nicknamed "Chevo" because he had a pet goat as a kid. He was our own "Fonzie" from happy days! He truly had the happiest laughter.

We also had our Uncle Ron, who was the jokester and always welcomed us with a joke. He was married to my mom's sister, and they were always fun to be around.

They'd come over to visit in their Ford Truck, with my cousins loaded in the back. Back then, it was allowed to ride in the bed of the truck and on the trail gate.

Uncle Ron would take his tennis shoes off and then get on his knees with the shoes sticking out from his knees as though he were a short-person comedian. He played the part so animated that he'd have all of us laughing in tears.

On one occasion, after a visit, we all went outside on the front porch to say "Goodbye" and wave them off, as we frequently did in the late evenings.

My cousins all piled onto the truck and waved, saying Goodbye until they were far down the street. We were still outside when we heard a vehicle honking as it passed by. It was my uncle and cousins again, and we laughed as we waved them off once again. Then, a few minutes later, we heard another honk. My uncle turned around, and they were all yelling "goodbye" and waving once again! He went around and around our short block before finally venturing home.

My uncle had a way of making memories that would last. It was hilarious to watch my uncle's truck with all my silly cousins in the back waving goodbyes over and over again with huge smiles like it was brand new!

It was a ritual for our family to get together, blankets and pillows in tow, in the back of my dad's Chevy pickup truck and go to watch movies at the drive-in theaters. Most often, it was the 40 Niner or Sunrise outdoor drive-in movie theater.

My dad would put the speakers in the back of his truck as we all nestled together with popcorn and snacks in our sleeping bags and blankets.

I could never make it to the end of the movie, and I would fall fast asleep. My parents would carry me into the house and tuck me into my bed. Probably because my favorite was playing around at the playground next to the snack bar, I would wear myself out!

My mother would also drop us kids off at the Foothill skating rink for their "all night" skate sessions. I would never be able to make it till morning and again would have to be carried out to the car and into my bed at home. I'd get worn out keeping up with my older siblings.

I recall my dad telling me that when I was born, the doctor dropped me right on my nose, and that's why my nose had a line down the middle.

He'd then take his 1st, 2nd, and 3rd fingers and clasp them lightly around my nose and pull them back, saying, "Rip the nose." Then he'd show me his thumb between those fingers as if it were my real nose, and I would chase after him until he gave me my nose back.

Ironically, my eldest brother accidentally dropped me when my mom brought me home from the hospital. Mom said he tried to swing me around and accidentally dropped me on the floor. I could gain sympathy from my brother by reminding him of this!

And it was a great thing that my nose did remain intact!

My eldest sister had a graffitied door in our bedroom. Every person or a new friend that came to visit was allowed into our room to mark their memory on this door by writing their name or a message, leaving the door covered from top to bottom with signatures, art, and creative graffiti. I wished we'd taken that door with us when we moved because it was truly a remarkable and memorable work of art.

My eldest brother found himself to have a green thumb. My sisters and I were not allowed in my brother's room. However, one day, my brother had his door wide open, and I could see inside. I was amazed that my brother was growing beautiful green plants with spotlights over them. Somehow, they managed to keep mom out of their room, too, by keeping it clean and changing their own linens and by managing their own laundry, which mom didn't mind because she worked long shifts at the nursing home at this time, and she'd often come home tired.

One day, mom did venture into their room, and I was surprised to hear her yelling in anger at my brother for growing these beautiful green plants, which were, in fact, marijuana plants, and my mother made him rip them to shreds and throw them into the garbage.

My brother was sad, but he knew to follow mom's rules, and truly, he wasn't looking to get into trouble. He and his friends thought they were cool, as most of the teen boys who hung around my brothers wore t-shirts with the plant print on them.

I wasn't impressed by them or their t-shirts, but I was mostly impressed with my brother's gardening skills.

Chapter 2

INTO THE LIGHT, BACK TO LIFE, BACK TO REALITY

Back to my story... I was getting back on my feet and finding my way in life. I was busy raising my children, working in the café, attending college, and volunteering in the church.

When I was 19 years old, men naturally began to notice me. Up to this point, my work toward healing began to show in physical and spiritual ways and in my perceptions, too. The fruits of my hard work were seen in the whole mind, body, and soul, and they became attractive.

Every part of my healing took time; the effort I put into it came with its own set of struggles and triumphs.

Many developmental milestones occur between the ages of 15 and 19. My natural growth was stunted, and therefore, I was at a loss for functioning effectively within society. Therefore, I became vulnerable and needed to relearn everything again. Making good choices in relationships was one huge obstacle.

I would love to have had a "fairytale ending" after coming out of my oppression. However, this was not my reality, as life had many lessons to teach `me along the way. God has always guided me, though, at times, I couldn't see it due to my human limitations. My life can serve as an example for others to follow.

The greatest gain I experienced along the way, not in spite of but because of my suffering, was the ability to experience true bliss and joy that embraced me completely.

The glory of a sunrise and sunset made me gasp in amazement and gratitude at their magnificence as tears streamed down my cheeks. They left me with feelings of awe and amazement at their beauty, brilliance, and glory.

Because I had lost so much of myself, I had learned to appreciate every gain and every moment of truest beauty and substance as revealed in nature.

I began to navigate through this life as an adult

and as a single parent. I started gaining new skills, making new friends, and hanging out with my peers, as it gave me immense pleasure. I cleared my schedule to include all these activities in my life. Because good babysitters were not easy to arrange, and I'd get caught up in time, I came up with a plan.

So, I'd entertain in my home like my own parents did. I'd cook delicious meals for everyone and have movie nights or swimming parties with my friends.

My sons got spoiled by my girlfriends, and they got to meet really good people who became like family.

Being a teen mom and a responsible adult was a huge challenge for me. Although I still longed to have fun and be free, I knew I had to prioritize my needs if I was to be successful.

Working part-time to pay the bills and attend college was a huge sacrifice, but I knew it was worth the effort.

I was determined to provide a good home for my sons and to better my life. We easily fell into a routine that included work, school, church, family, social lives, and home life. Juggling all these responsibilities proved worthwhile, as life was full of vibrancy, and we were surrounded by the love and support of family and friends.

I realized that it truly takes a village to raise children, to raise myself as a productive citizen, and to safely navigate through this life.

In addition to all those activities, I started going on dates. The youth minister at church showed interest in me by smiling when he saw me and taking a liking to my sons. He asked to baptize them in the church and stepped up to be their "Godfather" under the oath of God.

He became a trusted friend, and he was truly a good man from a great family. He was a kind and hard worker, owned his own home and company, and above all, he loved God.

He decided to offer me a blessing just as my father had offered to my mother that day when my father took my siblings & I to be his children.

One day, Felix decided he would propose to me

on a bent knee, with a diamond in his hand, in front of my family and friends; I became paralyzed with fear. I froze, not knowing what to do, so "fight or flight" took control, and I ran out of the house, leaving everyone in shock and disappointment.

Perhaps it was the idea of being "trapped" with no way out. The trauma I endured still lay fresh in my brain and heart, so I ran for my life.

I couldn't see the blessing due to my past trauma, and I was on the road to healing, and the last thing I needed was a stumbling block.

Now, I realize it was much worse than I can even recall. My body, my brain, my heart, and my spirit required healing, as this wouldn't be an easy fix. And every ounce of trauma I had endured added to the layers.

Now, I know there is always hope!

Next, I was at the café in deep thought when a tall, tan, handsome man with a huge pearly white smile approached the counter. He looked similar to "Ponch" Poncherrello in the police drama television series *CHIPS* in 1983. I always thought him cute.

He asked me my name and started small talk as he placed his order. Joey continued to pay visits to the café until one day, he asked me to join him on his fancy sports motorcycle for a ride through the park. I agreed to go, and the next day, he showed up with a gift box.

Up to this point, I knew little to nothing about big-name brands, expensive jewelry, or styles in the latest fashions. In fact, most, if not all, of my attire was gifted to me as used clothing or purchased at Goodwill as I did not have the funds to spare. Given the fact I had sons and myself to support.

Joey instructed me to go ahead and open the box. Inside lay my very first pair of designer "Guess" jeans with zippers up the sides of the ankles. He also gifted me a pair of blue and white "Reebok" tennis shoes to go along with them. He later added a small designer purse and a delicate watch for my wrist that matched his.

He further explained that it was nothing for him to purchase these things for me, and amazingly, everything fit perfectly. He wanted me to feel confident on the bike ride through the park, and I later came to realize it was a huge event, as his closest friends were there that day.

As he rode through the park, I sat on the back of his seat, feeling proud. He introduced me to his friends, and I felt like a million bucks that day.

The gifts he continued to lavish on me were extravagant, even allowing me to drive his new Hyundai to work, and he paid for the gas.

However, I felt that I was slowly drifting apart from the church and from my obligations there as I began to spend more time with Joey and his friends. He began to slowly control my world and led me down a path of material gains and a life where having a good time took precedence over his responsibilities. He was not abusive, but his lifestyle became destructive.

He treated my sons well, enjoyed cooking meals, and had a pleasant nature about him, but he was persuasive and extremely manipulative. I'd overhear his conversations with his mother. His parents were educated people who held respectable positions in their careers and in the community. His mother argued with him to "get his priorities in order," and he'd quiet her with promises he did not keep.

One evening, after we'd dated for a few months and were just hanging out, he handed me a cold glass of cola. I thought nothing of it and drank it down immediately, as it was a warm summer day, and I was thirsty. Next thing, my heart began to race out of my chest, and I thought I was having a heart attack; I was in a panic, not knowing what to do.

Little did I know Joey had spiked my drink with drugs, and this began my introduction to "the underworld." He told me to relax and that he wanted me to have some "fun." He apologized and assured me it would wear off. I made my way home, and by morning, I decided to go to the fire station near my home. They checked my vital signs and advised me to go home and get some rest. And if I didn't feel better, go to the ER.

I was young and naïve, and I should have put an end to the relationship right then and there, but I didn't. Joey began to take me to random people's homes whom he introduced to me as his "friends," and he'd leave me sitting in the living room as he ventured off to have conversations with them alone. I noticed that he began to look quite ragged.

At one point, we went to a "friend's" home, and for the first time in my life, I witnessed men and women shooting themselves up with heroin. It was at this moment my eyes were opened to the world of drugs and drug dealers. I was shocked by what I witnessed, and I KNEW right at that very moment that Joey had fallen deep into a dark, dark world of evil.

I began to distance myself as this last scenario truly frightened me to the core, and I knew this was not the type of people God called me to associate with!

On the night my drink was spiked, I began to hallucinate as I was unable to sleep for several days! I knew I had to make my way back to church. So, one evening, I joined my mom and our family friends at an event at a small church in our area where a female evangelist would be invited to give a Sermon.

The women prayed over me that evening and instructed me to completely cut ties with Joey, to which

I willingly complied.

I ignored his calls and, with the help of my family, moved out of my dwelling. I completely cut ties with him and his friends and never looked back.

God had once again rescued me due to my obedience & lessons learned.

I later learned that Joey had gotten himself involved with the wrong people and with women in their circles and began to go deeper into his corrupt lifestyle. He was found in an abandoned house, nearly beaten to death & left there for dead, unconscious for days.

I continued to pray for him, his recovery, and his salvation.

I never Saw him again, and through all of this, I learned that this lifestyle in the "fast lane" leads a person to a path of destruction as there is absolutely nothing good that can come from it.

I also realized how God was able to open my eyes by allowing me to see for myself what illegal drug abuse does to people & how it can start out slowly and then progress. The seemingly innocent person just wants to "have a little fun," but then it takes them further into a place of darkness where oftentimes there is no turning back and can potentially put their lives in danger and even to death.

It was at this point in my life that I was no longer naïve to the spiritual realms of God nor the darknesses in life.

My gifts of healing began at a young age in the church, and they have carried me through every trial I have faced and have yet to encounter.

At my young age, witnessing people strung out on drugs & hallucinating, I'd be there taking care of their children as I'd be the only one not using them and with a clear head.

One time, a friend was walking straight out into the traffic, and it was I who deterred her back to safety. I put her into a cold shower, and she was fully clothed. I gave her milk to drink and put her to bed. I watched after her children and put them to bed as everyone around me was on some "Trip."

God did not allow me to have the appetite to join them, as I used the excuse of "being Allergic" to substances.

God was there, & the healing gifts I learned were to take care of people and to have a heart for them. In this, I was allowed to take care of family & friends as they were nearly in an overdose of lethal substances.

Each person whom I accompanied and cared for in this manner during my youth knows their own experience, and I mention this not to single anyone out or ridicule them but rather to highlight that God had a "calling" on my life to minister healing to the sick and to those who need a healing touch.

God has a purpose for our lives, and in this, He allowed me first-hand training in order to raise me up with the experience and tools I'd require for the calling He had and has on my life. I'm grateful for every experience that trained me in the art of compassion and the art of being human.

Before, my brother was "Accidentally" shot and killed by his best friend at the young age of 18 with so much promise ahead of him. My mother had a real and unique encounter with God.

My Mother had committed her life to The Ministry and to the Works of God. My Dad, who was an Atheist, and Mom began to clash. Therefore, they each took to their own sides of their bed, refusing to snuggle. In fact, although they lay there together, they couldn't have been further apart, isolated and feeling alone.

One night, while Mom and Dad were asleep, my mother was suddenly jolted awake by a voice so powerful it shook the bed, waking both her and Dad. Mom began to speak in an "unknown language" as Dad watched in horror.

Mom was then yanked from the bed and onto her knees. As all this was happening, according to my father, he tried to reach out to shake her out of it, but as he reached out to touch her, there was an invisible wall or realm between them that his hand could not penetrate.

Dad later explained it as a barrier that prevented him from even touching Mom. Mom explained her experience as being abruptly shaken from her bed and onto her knees, where she heard the voice command, "Praise Me!"

Mom knew this voice without hesitation & replied, "No, God." She said, "Ever since I dedicated my life to you, I've experienced numerous troubles."

The Voice told her, "I am here to take your life."

Mom then pleaded for her life, explaining that she has children to take care of and that she knows she is not ready. I believe God was there to relieve her from the suffering she would soon endure.

The voice said, "Ok, then, this is your future."

A window suddenly appeared before her, and it was so foggy. She had to wipe the fog away when a silhouette of a male figure surfaced. Mom then pleaded to please reveal to her who this male figure was behind the fogged window. Instead, the voice said,

"I will be with you. I will give you strength."

Mom recalls waking up and looking like she'd just run a marathon but states, "I felt high in Spirit."

Dad was unusually silent that morning as he and Mom went about their daily activities. Mom finally broke the silence by saying, "We need to talk."

Mom made them each a cup of coffee & they sat together at our dining table to have a discussion as they each tried to make sense of what had happened. Dad then verified that Mom was suddenly shaking from the bed in some Sort of trance as she spoke some strange language that Dad did not understand. He attempted to reach out to her but couldn't, as there was an invisible wall between them preventing him from touching her. Dad was in shock as he simply could not make sense of what he'd witnessed.

My mother then walked across the street to my grandmother's house, for surely grandma had the wisdom to help mom make sense of what she'd experienced.

As she walked through the door, Grandmother exclaimed, "What happened to you?" My mother looked completely drained.

Mom told Grandma about her experience that

morning, and Grandmother advised Mom to prepare as someone in the family was going to die.

They didn't know who or when, and each believed it would be one of the uncles. Nobody could have prepared for the shock that shook our family to its core, especially Mom.

Within the next few days, Mom received the horrifying news that my beloved brother, with his beautiful, mild nature, was accidentally shot and killed by his best friend with his friend's father's hunting gun they'd found in his parent's attic. This was to become the first tragic death in our family, and nobody was prepared.

If it weren't for God on my Mom's side giving her the strength she needed in this dark hour. She'd surely not have made it through as God came to warn her and to reassure her that He would give her the strength she'd need to overcome as there would be more trials to come that would try us as a family, and my mother remained our rock just as her mother had before her and we all needed her for our survival.

Chapter 3

OPEN THE EYES TO MY HEART

I came to realize that my relationship with Joey was falling apart, and this was the reason I sought help from the church when I heard that a prophetess happened to be in town. My mother and our church friends picked me up and accompanied me to meet this woman of God, whose name was Laura.

This woman and her son, who had some physical disabilities, traveled across cities, ministering and spreading the word of God. Laura's son, Chuck, explained to all of us that his mother devoted her life to this work as she often spent hours in prayer in her "prayer closet."

Prophetess "Laura" prayed over me and began to prophesy. She started by sharing a scripture, Psalm 37, verses 1 through 40. This scripture was for me to meditate on as she informed me that God has a purpose for my life, that many messages of healing would come through me, and that many would fall on their faces because of the Word of God.

However, she emphasized that I should not take any credit for this as I would merely be used as the presenter, and God is the true author. She told me that God had sent his angels to cleanse my house and my life and urged me to walk away from this relationship without looking back.

She instructed me that God would direct me and assured me that my children would be blessed as God would use them for his honor.

I took her words to heart, and that's why I made the decision to move forward that very day and leave everything that needed to be left behind.

This part of my life seemed to be a very hard lesson for me, but I trusted that God would use that wisdom later in life as I made my way into His purpose for me.

I then got a job at a large dry-cleaning plant, where my mother worked as a floor supervisor. Due to my hard work and dedication, I was promoted to a secretary position. However, later, I faced disappointment as I was laid off due to budget cuts.

I was determined then to pursue a career in medicine. It was a choice that would ultimately prove to be the best decision I had ever made.

Then, I made the blunt decision to relocate to a town on the Upper East Side, away from my family and the people I'd previously encountered, seeking a fresh start.

Looking back now, I can see clearly that it was God who encouraged me to move and directed my steps.

I enrolled in a Career College in East Sacramento and graduated with a certification as a Medical Assistant.

After completing my studies, I secured a Position in a private Pediatric practice. I worked in this position for ten years, learning and carrying out responsibilities that built up my confidence & skills. I had the privilege of working side by side with the doctor and his wife, who graciously took me under their wings. They even encouraged me to get my RN license & made me believe in myself. I emulated their character and truly experienced success, stability, and happiness.

I enjoyed working with children and our staff. I was grounded, and it was during this time that I met my soon-to-be husband. We shared mutual acquaintances, and our relationship blossomed into a beautiful romance. It was a magical moment when he proposed to me in a quaint French restaurant in the city of Carmel, with large glass windows framing breathtaking views of mountains.

The waitress brought out a Chocolate dessert with one lit candle, and the hugest, sparkling diamond ring was shining in front of my eyes. This time, I accepted when he got down on one knee as the guests in the restaurant exploded in applause. I was truly happy, in love, and content.

My husband was a handsome and kind man. He was generous and a good provider. He was smart and humorous and took care of his health and his body, but he was not faithful.

I figured it out on a company picnic at a Water Park as I noticed a lady much younger than us flirting with my husband, and he flirted back. This whole drama carried on between them as I took mental notes!

We were deeply in Love, but it became apparent that he was a bit more in love with himself. His ego took over, and eventually, we grew apart. Apart from that, he provided me with everything I wanted; he, like my biological father, couldn't offer me the essential elements of complete love, loyalty, or total devotion that I longed for.

I turned to a minister I met on the internet who encouraged me to leave my husband. Neither one of us knew how to fight- to hold our marriage together, and therefore, it painfully came to an end. Consequently, he ended up marrying the same lady he was flirting with, who ended up being less than what he had expected. Later on, I heard that he accidentally called out my name and admitted that she did not carry the same outgoing and positive energy he had in me.

It was too late to realize that we already had the best in each other. I truly was in love with my husband, and this proved to be a very painful break. The hurt we endured and the trust that was broken was too great to repair. The break was permanent, and so was the friendship. Everything was permanently broken.

We had to divide assets, and right before I left our home, he and I bought brand new and built from the ground up. Before we parted ways, I was running on my treadmill one day in my bedroom and heard God in my mind talking to my heart. It was not an audible voice, but I *knew* it was God.

He said, "You must be strong! You will go through storms in your life, but I will be with you. Do not fear."

I got on my knees, and I cried. I cried for our loss, and I cried for me and my husband. I knew we were defeated. At one point, he and I held each other, and we both cried tears of sadness. I recalled him saying to me,

"I still love you, but this pain and the damage is too great."

We were too young and naïve and didn't know how to help ourselves. I took my portion of our divided assets, and I bought a home for myself and my sons in the city of Citrus Heights, CA. (This will later prove to have miraculous findings as I am later introduced to my roots.)

Here I was, once again, navigating through life as a single young mother without a compass. My home was close to work, so rain or shine, I was able to work hard to supply all my and my son's needs without assistance from anyone.

It was tough at times, but I was determined to make it, no matter the great sacrifices.

In hindsight, I did not even realize then that it was God who carried us through. That one thing that remained consistent in my life was my strong faith in God. I remained devoted to my volunteer position in the church, teaching Sunday School and attending church.

In turn, God remained faithful in my life, providing for our daily needs. It was nearly 12 years from the birth of my youngest son and my eventual escape from an abusive situation at age 19 years old.

I'd experienced the underworld and challenging relationships. I was still in the process of healing, and with a new experience in life came a new set of things to be healed.

I continued to attend college and work in private practice while raising my sons and navigating through life without a spouse or a mate.

I'd had a dream about the doctor I'd worked for, and early one morning, as we spoke between the partition that separated the front office from the back office, I'd begun to plan the work day.

I said,

"Dr. Aguilar, I had the strangest dream about you."

"Oh yeah," he replied, "Tell me about your dream."

I went on to explain that in the dream, he was telling all of us that he was closing his doors. The office and all the staff will no longer work together in his office because his doors are closing. In the dream, there were lots of tears and sadness."

Dr. Aguilar looked straight into my eyes without saying a word and walked away. I thought, *"Okay, I just proved to him that I am crazy."* And I continued with our day. It was very busy at the end of our workday. Finally, as we were finishing up, Dr. Aguilar called me into his private office and asked me to have a seat. He went on to ask me who leaked this information to me about him closing his doors because nobody at this point had the knowledge besides himself and his wife that he was, in fact, on the verge of closing his office due to bankruptcy. I was in shock!

He said either you are extremely gifted, or you have tapped my home phone because that is exactly what has happened. I was going to inform all of you next week, but since you seem to know, I will tell you now.

Not everyone can come with me to my new facility as I am merging with another company, and I know the rest of the staff will definitely be devastated. I'd already planned on taking you and a few others with me. Please, at this point, keep this information private until I am able to talk to the staff.

I replied, "Yes, sir, I pleaded that it was a dream that I had no idea meant anything at all and that it would be my privilege to join you in your new location."

Once again, I was in awe of God but still not aware of how to utilize this gift in prayer for the strength of those it may affect. Later, I'd learn these valuable keys to utilizing prophecy for the best outcomes for all.

It has taken me many years to embrace the graces of God. I rationalized the fact that it is possible for me to pray and talk to a sovereign God through prayer. So, what makes me think He cannot also talk to me?

This realization of God's truth would continue to develop, as you will see through the years. It was during this period that I met my next-to-be spouse. I was in school to obtain an RN degree, and the pediatric office had indeed closed its doors, so I joined our doctor at his new clinic across town south of Sacramento. It was challenging for me as I'd gotten comfortable with our little "family" of coworkers and had my routine.

I'd begun an internship program partnering with the community colleges in the area. I'd interview, train, and prepare newly graduated Medical Assistants for their adventures in medicine.

I partnered with drug reps in our region and approved the samples we'd stock and supply to our patient clientele. I partnered with Vaccines for Children and was the contact who provided statistics and ongoing regulations in order to stock the vaccines provided and to vaccinate medical and sliding scale covered individuals in order to provide vaccines to all children in our region whom we served.

I loved my career and our office families. My coworkers were the best, and we were more like family than mere co-workers.

Dr. Aguilar and his wife had a baby who succumbed to his illness and was buried to rest with all of us present. The Dr. and his wife were truly the epitome of "good people," and I wanted to be just like them. I wanted to be a good person, too. So, I emulated their lives and tried my hardest to be "a good citizen" and a good person. They encouraged me to further my education, and so I did.

Chapter 4

A VISITING ANGEL ENCOUNTER

Jaxon worked at the clinic as a mental health worker and social worker, assisting with patient care and outpatient needs. Our paths crossed, and he initiated a gradual pursuit of a closer relationship with me. Eventually, he found the courage to ask me out to the movies. At first, I hesitated and started giving the excuse that due to my demanding schedule and commitment to nursing school studies, I couldn't come.

He continued to ask, and eventually, I relented, telling myself, *"What would it hurt?"* As we spent time together, we clicked, and I discovered him to be intelligent, interesting, fun, energetic, outgoing, and well-informed. In short, he was different than the rest. He brought a fresh perspective to life, challenging me to open my view of society and reassess my perspectives.

Over time, I adopted this perspective and became seasoned in this way of thinking, particularly during one of my sociology courses in college. One fine day, the professor approached me and said, "Tina, may I have a word with you?"

He began to express his concern with the assignments I'd submitted for review. He pointed out that I seemed to be holding back and not producing the excellent essays he had expected from me, given that he was already familiar with my writing style.

I tried to explain my challenge and mentioned that my religious upbringing made it difficult for me. It'd be challenging for me to accept certain things, such as the cultural practices in which men dressed up as women & even so far regarded as "Royalty." I explained my fear that if I took on such beliefs, the entire foundation of my upbringing would crumble.

Suddenly, his face lit up, and he came up with a brilliant idea. He said, "For the sake of learning, just pretend you are putting on a pair of invisible glasses. These glasses allow you to see through temporary lenses in order to view the world through another person's eyes. That way, you can broaden your perspective & expand your mind. When you are done, simply take off the glasses & perceive things as normal again." I embraced this school of thought wholeheartedly, and as a result, I graduated with Honors.

This perspective became my approach to life from that day on, which enabled me to communicate with Jaxon on an agreeable level.

Our Meeting ultimately led to our marriage, and

it was so unfortunate that our first daughter passed away before she could come into this world. This happened in my last trimester of pregnancy. I could sense that something was terribly wrong. Urgently, I asked my husband to drive me to the hospital. When we arrived there, a nurse administered a muscle relaxant and monitored the baby for less than an hour. Shockingly, without a word from the Doctor, I was sent home. I was reluctant to go home while explaining to the nurse that I still felt that something was wrong.

That night on my birthday, I felt my baby's kick for the very last time. The medication took hold, and I drifted into a deep sleep. And as I felt myself slipping far away, I whispered please, "Stay."

By the time I was so weak and blacking out, I begged my husband to take me back to the hospital. I could barely find enough energy to speak. My abdomen was cramping into a tight contraction as I felt my mind slipping in and out of consciousness.

We made it back to the hospital. When the Doctor entered the room and delivered the devastating news that my baby was "gone," All I could hear was some heart-wrenching cries of a grieving woman from a far away and distant place. She was screaming, "No God! Please, God! No!" and my heart ached for her.

Her Voice sounded like my own, yet at that very moment, I couldn't be sure of anything real, not even my own existence.

Our daughter was born perfect, with pink, rosy, supple cheeks and beautiful dark, curly locks of hair. Although she was lifeless, she looked like a perfect Angel.

The grief struck me so hard that I doubted I'd survive it. None of it made any sense. However, I was a healthy individual who worked out at the gym regularly. I jogged and ate healthy. I took vitamins and avoided alcoholic drinks. I didn't smoke tobacco or take any illegal drugs, and I didn't require prescription medications. I was so angry at my circumstances, and I took it out on God.

I couldn't understand how I could do so much right and still experience so much Wrong. I cried out to God, and still, I had no good answers. One evening, I gained the courage to call the "Dr. Laura" radio show to ask her a pressing question, "I had a 10 % chance that the same thing would happen again if I tried for another child just the way I'd lost my precious baby girl." Dr. Laura put me on the air and then advised me, "You have a 90% chance of your baby surviving." Her words resonated with me and so I prayed about it.

One evening, as I was asleep, l saw a dream of a girl child. She was wearing a ballerina-type dress. Away in the distance, accompanied by a female guardian as they made their way together down a pathway toward me. The child was happily twirling and twirling toward me. I was standing next to a broken-down car with the door open, and as she approached me, I called her by my daughter's name, whom I had recently lost. I received the answer, "No," as I approached the child to hug and hold her, and although she was happy, she was stern and focused. I felt lots of love. The guardian stood close by, watching over the child silently. I then heard a voice say, "This is your future. Do you accept?" As soon as the thought of agreement appeared in my being, I awoke,

I knew that every little detail in my dream had a significant meaning, including the broken-down car.

I later told my husband. "We will have a daughter. I met her in heaven, already in my dream." He did not know how to respond as we'd both been grieving the loss of our daughter.

Then, something unexpected happened. I realized that my monthly period was late. So, I took a pregnancy test and found out that, I was positive.

I had a Perinatologist who monitored the baby &

very closely delivered at 34 weeks, healthy and perfect! My beautiful Daughter spent a week in the ICU, and I spent several days in the hospital, but it was all Worth it!

She was born healthy & beautiful. When I was pregnant, I read to her & played classical music. When she was born, I bought her encyclopedias, and she knew the names of exotic animals. She speaks two languages. God has His hands on my beautiful daughter as He knows how to give good gifts to His children.

I was blessed with a child, but unfortunately, the marriage fell apart as my daughter's father held secrets that no wife wanted to know about. Due to this, an ugly battle raged over our child and over the divorce. We fought long and hard, and finally, my dream came to pass.

My little ballerina would spend her life shuffling back and forth in a vehicle that would remain concrete and stuck. The doors would remain open, and in it all, God's Angel guided and watched over us.

It was truly one of the most difficult areas of my

life to come to grips with losing my child and then being blessed with our beautiful daughter, only to watch things fall apart.

The hurt at times became unbearable, and at times, I felt truly abandoned by God. Grieving it all was the worst & just opening my eyes at times felt like a chore.

The attacks that followed from those who knew my ex-husband added an extra layer of burden, and just as I had the strength to get back up, I was once again knocked back down. I was misunderstood because I chose to keep my personal struggles with my spouse to myself, saving us all dignity. My daughter deserved this at Best!

This journey is still a battle, coming to terms with all the lost time with my daughter. We have made it through despite all the hardships. My daughter turned out to be a well-rounded individual and loved by all her family.

Although I "felt" like God was punishing me. Now, I know that everything I endured was for the good of those around me.

My failed relationships made it a struggle not to take things personally. Children are a true blessing from the Lord. In His mercy and grace, I have been blessed.

I recall the times in church when we'd imitate Christ by washing one another's feet.

Christ is King, and yet He humbled himself to a servant.

He had everything yet gave it all up to gain us,

his children, to have a loving family who would love him back. He sacrificed His own flesh for it, and this is the cost of love- sacrifice – we sacrifice for love, and, in the experience, we understand the truest meaning of it, for there is no such thing as love without sacrifice.

Even in failed relationships, the blessing is that we have experienced love. What an accomplishment for a mere man that we could experience love. This in itself is a Miracle!

The love of parents for their children is perhaps the closest man will ever get to understanding the devotion and love of God toward man. The term agape best describes it; for in all these things, Christ proves that I am truly loved.

John 3:16,

"For God So Loved the World That He gave His Only Begotten Son that whosoever believes in Him would not perish but have eternal Life."

Chapter 5

EXPERIENCING MIRACLES, SIGNS, AND WONDERS

"If you went back and fixed all the mistakes you have made, you erase yourself."

~ Louis C.K.

Here I stand once again, single. This time, my children have grown, and I have become more resilient than before.

My children always share our most cherished memories together, like Rollerblading, weekend sleepovers at our house with Blockbuster movies as I cooked some of their favorite foods & desserts, and watching people at Sunrise Mall.

I remember the times I'd show up at their school with McDonald's for lunch and the time we had spent together with extended family. We didn't have a lot of "Things," but we had each other, and we made sure to make those moments memorable and joyful.

Holding good memories in my heart and

enduring pain from the past- I finally graduated college with a license as a Registered Nurse. I was determined to accomplish something for myself.

However, during my career, I have encountered several Angels. Seems impossible? But it's true. As I cared for the most vulnerable at the end of their lives, I began to experience & accept miraculous encounters with The SPIRIT World. I have literally felt that the energies shift in the room when individuals are near those moments before and at death.

I had the privilege of taking care of a lovely lady during the stages of her illness. One day, in the final days of her life, she beckoned me to come close as she wanted to say something. Her eyes were filled with unspoken urgency. As I leaned in, she looked up at me and whispered, "Can you feel him? Can you feel God? He is so close I can feel His breath upon my face." Tears glistened in her eyes as she said this. Without any hesitation, I replied, "YES, I CAN."

Another elderly person was twisted up as a pretzel with contractures, as we call it. It is a condition in which the bones & muscles lose their ability to stretch. Upon entering his room, I immediately felt a Divine presence, knowing he was close to crossing over. With no family by his side, he lay alone in his bed in a large, spacious room all to himself. I began to speak softly and offered prayers over the person. I then gave him a warm, comforting bath and massaged his tightened muscles with lotion. Recalling hymns that I learned in church, I felt that familiar sensation of spirit as goosebumps rose on my skin and the hairs on my arms and neck tingled with this Divine energy.

Then I thanked this person for their contributions in this life & I gave this person permission to either stay awhile or to go ahead and let go when they are ready. I knew this dying person's spouse had passed on, and I reassured this individual that their spouse would be waiting, so we'd better get their dancing shoes on because they would soon be together and they would have a lovely dance. All of a sudden and without any warning, this dying person's body straightened out to its normal state. It felt like the body had completely healed miraculously!

The housekeeper, who coincidentally spoke the

same language as the patient, walked into the room right at that exact moment, and both she and I gasped in amazement. She'd developed a fondness for this patient. As his family had grown weary and decided to go home to rest, the housekeeper had taken it upon herself to check in on the patient from time to time. She had formed a unique bond with this patient. What we'd just witnessed was unbelievable. That morning, as I left my shift and walked out the door, this patient passed away. Both my coworker & I still discuss this miraculous experience as we shared it with this lovely person.

These encounters represent just a small part of the honorable moments I have been blessed to experience in my career. Without my own sufferings and struggles, I would not be able to fully understand the suffering of others. It is through these trials that I have developed empathy and compassion, which have allowed me to better connect with those during their most vulnerable moments.

With great compassion, I dedicate myself to serving others. With great gratitude, I approach each interaction & with embracing the greatest sacrifice; I am humbled by each & every experience. I give myself fully to this extremely self-sacrificial art of healing.

Chapter 6

COVID 19 HITS HARD

When COVID-19 hit in 2019, before any of us had gotten sick, thinking it was the flu, I lost my taste and smell, which is common with the common cold. The difference was that my body ached right down to the bone as though I were being stabbed with an ice pack. I struggled with shortness of breath and barely could walk as I didn't have the energy to get out of my bed. I felt as though my whole body was trapped beneath an enormous pile of building debris.

I took ten days off from work, and when I returned, I still had a lingering cough that would not go away, no matter what remedy I would use.

Shortly after, I gave myself time for distraction; I went on a vacation for almost a month in December. Upon coming back from vacation, when I entered the hospital, I was struck by an otherworldly sight - I saw my coworkers donned in Hazmat suits, resembling astronauts, protecting themselves against COVID. It was as if I had stepped onto another planet, akin to a scene straight out of the Twilight Zone.

I took it as a severe exaggeration until I was assigned to our COVID-19 SHELL UNIT to work directly with COVID-19-infected patients. We frontline workers were shocked and frightened as we reported for duty, feeling hopeless and at a loss for words as we witnessed what was happening around us.

Our stability was shaken as our worldviews took on an entirely new meaning. We encountered a vulnerability we'd not known until now as an entire healthcare system, and society got jolted with the shock of it. We all had to come together for one cause, and that was to annihilate what was destroying us! We went to war by realizing and embracing humility in the understanding of how much we relied on one another.

Every career, every position, and every part of our lives, even our children and all around the globe, were affected by this pandemic. As with any traumatic event, it brought out the Good, the bad, and the ugly in humanity.

We have only just begun to fully understand the

true meaning of being human and how each of us, great and small, plays a part and a major role in this particular thing that we call life!

Not one single human was left out of this equation as we all learned even the value of toilet paper! Who could have guessed that in 2019, the stock market couldn't even predict the value of a single roll of toilet tissue?

We were forced to be in this together. And just as human nature would have it, we did what we do best. We complained, and we pointed our fingers at one another, and we became hostile and violent, all the while thousands upon thousands lost their valuable lives, young and old.

Still, many of us did pray.

On a daily basis, we lost coworkers, family, and friends, and many people left the healthcare system completely, leaving the rest of us in a shortage, exhausted, and in a desperate state; many of us felt isolated as we were forced to stay away from people due to us being exposed. The irony of the situation was that we were forced to be isolated, and yet, deep down, we needed one another.

Many of us frontline workers were left with no better option than to seek out counseling and get on antidepressants to cope. We stuck it out collectively, and eventually, we came together. We voluntarily followed the rules, expertise, and suggestions, and we finally Overcame!

I was fortunate enough to work in our vaccine station, giving vaccines to our students and employees to combat COVID-19. I was also one of many reluctant to get the vaccine! Why, you would ask? Although I work in the health care system directly with those affected by this deadly virus, I was scared—straight up! Scared Witless!

My auntie, who is a retired nurse and also an expert in risk management and quality assurance, talked sense into me. She made me realize the benefits greatly outweigh the risks as I was directly face to face with this monster labeled 'COVID-19.'

This was not as easy a task as it should have

seemed. I sat outside the door for my appointment to get the vaccine. All of a sudden, my heart began to race wildly, and I felt as though I would puke. Without thinking rationally, I stood up and literally walked out. What happened next was nothing short of a miracle, as I was asked to volunteer some of my time to help out in giving the vaccines to my coworkers, hospital staff, and college students.

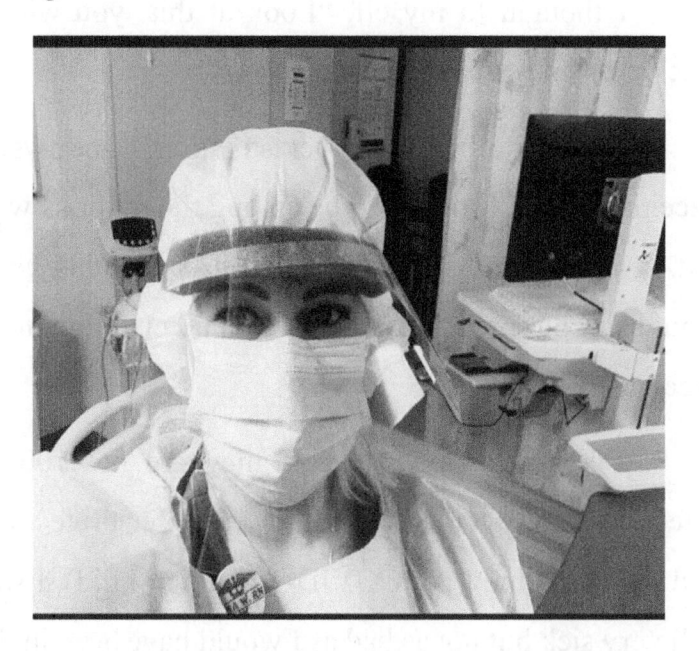

I agreed! As I inoculated those who had even more reason for concern, I listened to story after story of my coworkers who were currently battling cancer and those who were survivors of every sort, including our doctors. They explained to me that this was a brave act not only to help ourselves but also to aid society in beating this challenge.

Some got vaccinated because they worked with the most delicate and vulnerable patients, and they wanted, most of all, to protect themselves and, in turn, protect the vulnerable.

I thought to myself, "Look at this, you wimp! Buckle up and get vaccinated!"

So, after a massive procrastination, I got myself vaccinated, and I'm glad to be among the millions who did. It is quite possible that if we had not, this virus would still be spreading at all forces and claiming more precious lives.

Like with any vaccines, they are not 100 % effective against viruses, but they do offer protection, and the next time I got COVID-19 (which I did), I was still very sick but not as bad as I would have been in the first place when I'd not been vaccinated.

We are still treating those who get infected, but most have much less severe symptoms due to our collective efforts. I give each and every person credit for this because together, even in isolation, we got through it!

I offer my heartfelt prayers and deepest condolences to my family members, friends, coworkers, and patients who lost their lives during this tragic battle with an unknown virus that took us all by surprise. Every day, frontline workers bravely showed up in order to heal mankind. You, each, are truly honored, and I tip my nurse cap to you!

We now fully grasp the notion that we live in a world full of unpredictability, in which no one really knows what tomorrow may bring.

The best we can do is to live fearlessly and embrace this life we have.

We can experience and cherish every single moment with anticipation for the good. We can approach each day eagerly to spread acts of kindness and humility.

The Bible states that it is truly better to give than receive, and we can always allow opportunities to spread acts of kindness, no matter how great or how small. If it were our last opportunity, what would you like to be known for? Let us aspire to do great things and look for opportunities to spread love and kindness.

I have personally been a witness to such acts of kindness as I have worked side by side with professionals who have arranged for the homeless to provide comfort in their last days of life by letting them stay in a room or shelter. At the same time, they receive medications to comfort them in their final hours and then to provide a burial and plot with a plague because their lives are valuable.

I have witnessed the caring work of people who have arranged for a daughter to say her final "Goodbye" to her mother face to face during COVID-19, which was not allowed at that time. This mom and daughter had a moment together for the last time as her mom took her last breath, and her daughter was right beside her, holding onto her mother's hands.

I have also stood amongst physical angels who arranged for a loved one to die with dignity when pain and lack of breath were the alternate options.

I have stood amongst these saints who have literally given all they have to pull homeless people out from under a bridge to provide them shelter and comfort at the end of their lives.

I have stood beside doctors, providers, and caretakers who cry with you and for you because they are human, too. They carry the hearts of mankind in their hands and, too many times, try as they may. It is often out of their control whether life can be saved or not.

I don't believe that any professional who enters the miraculous field of medicine would ever think of naming themselves a "Hero," but that is exactly who they are: "Truly gifted heroes."

You save one life; you are a hero. You save hundreds upon thousands; you are a healthcare professional.

I am honored and amazed every day I get the chance to be a part of this community of healers. With every setback and every aspect of my own personal agony and suffering, I am becoming a true warrior of compassion, resilience, and humility.

Our truest training comes on the battlefield, for it exposes what and who you are in the rawest way and exposes what you are made of. How can I fight effectively if I am not first prepped for the battlefield?

In all of this, I thank my Lord above for knowing exactly what it would take to get me through this life and at the right exact time.

I have been brought down low, low, in humility, and in this humility, I have gained compassion, as it is here through this compassion alone that I am helpful to my fellowman without any of my own natural judgment.

It is with the help of my hidden power and strength, who is God Almighty, that I am able to approach life with an open heart. I am vulnerable yet available and able to receive this higher calling for the work of healer.

It is the power of surrender that allows me to grasp the truth that, in human form, we are much limited. In mind, body, and soul, just as in the rhymes, rhythms, and melodies of ode songs, I am able to dance to the tune of my own redemption song as I surrender to a power much higher than my own capabilities. I take this spirit of God by the hand in victories overcome by adversities as we dance in harmony to the flowing masterpiece called "Life."

Chapter 7

THE IMPORTANCE OF MENTORS

All my successes in life are the direct result of mentors God sent along my path to encourage me.

Starting at a very young age with my first Sunday School teacher.

"Mr. Good Bar" was our nickname for the man who offered to pick us kids up for Sunday School in his van each Sunday. He was an older and kind gentleman with a bald head. He was consistent, and oftentimes, on Sundays, Mom kept me home as I cried, not wanting to go.

On one of these occasions, with much coaxing from Mom, I finally gathered up the courage to join the other kids in the van. One particular Sunday, the Sunday School teacher offered us kids the Gift of Salvation, which I eagerly received. She welcomed us with a warm smile and open arms. This was one of my very first mentors in life. She shared stories of hope and redemption and taught us about the power of faith and the love of God. I was in preschool, as I remember, and what a powerful witness this woman was.

Another mentor was my Junior High School's Math Teacher. She was an elderly blonde-haired lady who piled all her hair high up into a bun. Through tiny glasses, she looked me right into my eyes and said,

"My dear, you will surely become a beauty knockout, but more importantly, get your education."

Those words remained with me throughout my life. When I found out I was pregnant at age 15, I turned to the free health clinic for prenatal care. There, a midwife cared for my well-being and imparted invaluable wisdom with each visit.

At every appointment, without fail, she would gently remind me, *"Get your education whenever and if ever you get the opportunity."* These messages continued to replay themselves throughout my life and became a constant refrain guiding my path.

Dr. Aguilar repeated these words to me as well throughout my work days in his clinic. He'd say, *"What do you have to lose but Time? It will pass regardless, so you may as well work on your education."* His words deeply affected me and resonated with my spirit.

Ironically, the first step I took after breaking free from five years of seclusion and abuse was to get a good education. I pursued my High School diploma and enrolled in City College. I was as determined as anyone to succeed. Despite the scars of my past, I refused to give up. With education as my solid foundation, I embraced every opportunity to rebuild my life, brick by brick. I surrounded myself with successful people & I emulated their lives.

I grew up in a hardworking family where women married at a very young age, dedicated themselves to raising families, and diligently managed their homes. My mother was more concerned with putting food on the table & paying the bills. Basically, living to survive. Grandmother firmly believed that a woman should not be alone, and Mom took on the belief that "The Way to a man's heart was through his tummy." She'd say this to my sisters and I: "No man wants a lazy woman who can't cook." Therefore, Mom instilled in us the essential skills to become capable and nurturing wives - *good wives.*

In my family, my mother's sisters were esteemed for having "Married Well," as they did not need to work outside their homes. Their primary role was caring for their husbands and their children, and their home was only the right place for them to be.

Women were encouraged to be of noble character— a good steward, a good mother, a loving wife, and a great homemaker.

However, as time moved forward, both women and men had to work just to keep up with the rising economy and cost of living. The situation shifted as it demanded both women and men to enter the workforce in order to sustain themselves. This change challenged the previous ideology and traditional gender roles and expectations, reshaping the dynamics of family and work life.

As the pressures of modern life intensified, the prevalence of single-parent households increased, pushing more women into the workforce. Education became a vital tool for survival, especially for achieving a comfortable standard of living. Ultimately, this shift meant that children were left to become "Latchkey kids," coming home to empty houses after school.

This trend contributed to a downward spiral in common ethics, which gave rise to behavioral problems as children were left without much-needed Parental guidance and care. The absence of parental guidance left a void that was often filled with negative influences, further exacerbating the challenges faced by families and communities.

So, was the case with me. I also came to realize that I'd need a sufficient career to provide for myself and my children, securing their future. I had no help as I did it all alone, and in fact, I also supported my young son, who was in my mother's care, as I navigated through life as best I could.

I had immense responsibilities and multiple roles to juggle, leading to many sleepless nights as oftentimes I studied until the wee hours of the morning. I knew I could handle it with God on my side, and therefore, giving up was never an option! I kept telling myself,

"Be strong, you've got this."

I recall a particularly busy work day when a middle-aged man walked into our clinic. As I took his blood pressure, he shared with me that he was a War Veteran. Despite his age, he seemed far too young to have experienced such trials. As he sat on the treatment table, he exposed his arm, and there, in huge bold letters, He bore a tattoo that read, "BE STRONG." It seemed to scream at me, and as he left, never to return, he left a bold imprint in my mind. I wondered if he was a messenger because, to this day, that tattoo is buried in my brain, and the image resurfaces when I feel Low, Weak, or Defeated. It continues to give me strength as I repeat, "Be Strong."

In My Youth at Church one Sunday evening, a well-known Prophetic Man prophesied over me as he said, *"Tina, you will make it very far in this life. God wants you to know that Satan is going to try to steal your joy. Do not let him! Stay close to God & He will fight for you. Just believe it and put your trust in God."* I've never forgotten these words.

When my precious baby daughter died, I was

back at work after I'd used up all my bereavement time off. An older gentleman came into the clinic and said, "Young lady, why do you look so sad?"

I told him I'd recently lost my baby and still did not understand how or why. This older man went on to explain to me the balance of life's Scales.

"There is a time to live and a time to die, and those times vary for each human on earth. The scales must remain balanced. Each of us has a time for our missions to be fulfilled. It seems to me your little one fulfilled her mission to be your angel." His words brought tears to my eyes and a truth to my heart.

I began to understand the meaning of True love and loss. I'd gone to personal counseling during this period of time & the counselor wanted to try art therapy with me.

She asked me to draw from my heart and not my mind. What surfaced was a piece of art so profound that it brings me chills even now when thinking about it.

I painted a mixture of light and dark-colored pictures, one side so dark as to symbolize death and the other an array of bright and glorious colors symbolizing life and life ever after.

The Counselor then asked me to interpret the drawing. I told her that my precious baby daughter has gone on to Glory, where there is only joy, Love, and abundant life.

The other dark side is dreary, and here, it is difficult to breathe; there is sadness and gloom, and the light has completely gone out.

She asked me, "Who resides there?!!"

I told her, "Here, in this dark place, is where I reside." She looked at me in deep thought and then carefully and softly said, "Then who is it that has died?" Her words hit me like a brick & that day, I decided that I would live.

During my divorce from my daughter's father, we were instructed to go to counseling together and then independently.

During one of those sessions, I exposed my past to the counselor after many sessions & after much sharing of deep emotions, as is the root of good therapy work.

Surprised at myself for digging up such memories, I lifted my head and looked up to find my counselor with tears in his eyes. The counselor took a moment to gain his composure & said, "If I could, I would hold you in my arms like my own child & rock you- NOT in any strange or disrespectful way but in a caring way, Tina; I want you to know & really understand how brave you are. The one strength that will get you through is that you do not give up." These words are etched in my mind, and again, I repeat them over & over as they also give me strength in trying times.

God, my Father, who knows me even better than I know myself. He knew exactly who to send at the right time and exactly what to say with the exact right words of encouragement to get me through this life.

When I came out of the relationship with the "Ponce, from chips" look-alike and went to the Church service where the Prophetess called me up to the altar to tell me that "God is going to use you in a Mighty way to speak His words of Truth and to get His message out

& that's why you have endured Such suffering.

People Will Mistake it for a human gift, and they Will fall on their faces before You because of what comes out of you, but it will not be because of you but because of the Spirit of God within you." She said, "Stay humble and let God be glorified. And please, don't give up!"

Through her words and my relentless faith, I know that God will be with me to get me through—no matter what comes my way—as long as I continue to have faith, believe in Him, and trust Him with my life. I truly do. I know that His Love, Kindness, and mercies toward me endure, and they are always for my good—but always for His glory.

Chapter 8

SPIRITUALITY & SPIRITUAL THINGS

My grandmother was a true *Demon Slayer*, much like "Buffy the Vampire Slayer," alongside my uncle and other family members who assisted her in exercising the demons that were haunting people's lives and their dwellings.

My grandmother had a unique gift of casting out evil spirits. She, my uncle, and, at times, my mother would fast and pray to prepare for this work. Grandma took this task very seriously and expressed the importance of being fully prepared for this level of intense work. My mother would later share with us some of the experiences they'd encountered, as my grandmother never freely spoke about it.

During one of these sessions, my grandmother, uncle, mom, and a church friend were asked to come to a home for a cleansing. Mom said it got so intense that my grandmother made my mother and her friend wait outside because the situation became too dangerous. The walls apparently started moving during this ritual. I took it as the battle got so intense the walls shook.

My grandmother was one of those rare individuals that everyone wanted to be around. Her positive energy was infectious! I've not met many people like my grandmother. She epitomized strength, love, and gentleness, all gracefully bundled into one. My grandmother lived and breathed for our family, and we lived for her.

Grandma was a down-to-earth personality who could see into the spiritual realms. She often encountered angels and interpreted dreams. One of her qualities that stood out among others was that she spoke with wisdom and common sense, which is rarely common in people.

Her spiritual gifts were genuine, and our family, the community, and our church family honored her. She was greatly loved and respected. She was devoted, loyal, and a person one could count on for support. Grandma was humorous without effort, and we were all blessed and so very lucky to have her as our mom and grandmother.

On one occasion, we'd all attended a church service and invited extended family, cousins, and their significant others. As our minister got deep into his sermon, a loud noise started coming from the back pew of the Church. A woman began to growl and curse. The pastor requested his deacons to escort the lady to the altar. As they did, the lady began to struggle and curse, spit, and scratch.

The lady fell to the ground at the altar, and our pastor warned the Church to open their Bibles and begin to pray. I was upfront with my mom because she played the tambourine and sat up front. The lady was in full view. Her belly was moving up and down like a snake. Her eyes were rolled back, and strange, deep voices echoed out from her.

She cursed obscenities, scratched at the pastor's face, and spit at him. She appeared to be foaming out of her mouth but without any signs of seizures. I recognized the foaming because I had seen it before when my older sister had seizures, but this woman wasn't experiencing a seizure. Something rare was happening to this woman, and we were witnesses to this rarity.

The next thing I knew, my cousins, their girlfriends, and my siblings were rushing out of that Church. They vowed never to return as they were thoroughly spooked!

However, this disturbing scene that played itself out before our very eyes and ears should have instilled some fear in me. I was not afraid, but instead, I held my Bible open and I prayed. Eventually, the lady was moved to a back room of the Church, and a team of church members, including my mom's friend, stood overnight at the Church to exercise the demons out of this lady.

By morning, they succeeded, and she was fully delivered. According to my mom's friend, it was discovered that the lady had gotten herself deeply involved in practicing the black magical arts and had picked up some powerful, dark, evil spirits. She didn't recall what happened to her that evening until after she was delivered. It was apparent she went into some deep trance as whichever spirits she had conjured up into possessing her had been released and set free by the mighty powers of God through the rituals of prayers over her by the elders of the Church, and it took all night to do so.

This was the first time I'd ever encountered something like this. Now, I am certain that it was real as there is no way to make all that up, even for the most skilled actors. That lady became a faithful and dedicated member of the Church and never returned to that dangerous cult. I still had to keep myself from obviously staring at her from time to time, thinking, "Wow, you had real demons talking out of you!" That's insane. I was thankful for her that she received deliverance before she encountered irreversible troubles. God is gracious and so good!

He warns us against these practices and such things for a good reason. We cannot control the perfect and complete will of God nor try to force his all-capable hands to "make" things happen by conjuring up evil entities. We certainly cannot win nor gain any good from it, and We cannot control God, for He knows what is best for each of us, and this serves as our lesson to "Trust God With All Our Hearts And To Lean Not On

Our Understandings." It is the surest way to steer clear of troubles.

"God advises us to set our minds and hearts on things above that are good and not on the things of the earth that offer only temporary value."

~Colossians 3:2

Not only was I mentored by the people God sent to me in my life through eye-opening experiences, but I've also been mentored by God himself, who helped me understand and embrace His truths, which set me free. Through His guidance, I learned the consequences of disobeying His Word of Truth and why it is so damaging to disregard it by following my own desires, especially in knowing they can be detrimental to my good.

I'm learning to learn and trust in the guidance God offers through His Wisdom.

My family was rooted in Christianity. Things were not always perfect, and neither were we, for in order to be perfect, it would mean for us to be Almighty God, and in all our imperfections, there is room for each of us to grow. This is what life is all about, in its essence: learning from our circumstances and from each other. This feeling makes us human. It teaches us how to be humane by opening our hearts to one another, and in this, we offer our gifts to deliver lives out of darkness and into the wondrous light. All it takes is a willingness to receive. In receiving, we may also learn to give of ourselves to others in need until kindness is spread far and wide as we evolve into all God created us to be. In turn, it returns us back home to where only our hearts reside. This is love in its natural state, expressed through actions.

*****

Familial rituals can be considered part of that unity of natural Love in action. My Uncles played musical instruments and liked to gather family and friends together to sing. My grandfather played the harmonica and also loved to sing. They'd gather with harmonica, conga drums, guitar, and accordion, and we'd gather on grandmother's porch to sing Gospel. Oftentimes, ranchera music filled the air with song and laughter.

My uncles purchased vans to Caravan to Church. They'd pick up Grandma first, then our group, including my cousins, & often our family friends. We were packed to the brim in our seats, with some sitting way in the back of the van on the floor as we sang our way to Church & back home. I could still hear my grandmother singing with all her heart, *"Todos deben de saber quién es Jesús. Él es el lirio de los valles. Él es la rosa de Sarón. Él es el astro esplendoroso. Todos deben de saber."*

Translation: Everybody ought to know who Jesus is. He's the Lily of the Valley. He's the rose of Sharon. He's the bright morning star. He's the fairest of ten thousand to my soul. Everybody ought to know.

My grandmother was a Strawberry blonde with striking blue eyes and pale skin. My Mom says her friends would tell her, "That's not your mom! That lady is an Oakie," which is a descendant from Oklahoma or a "White" migrant, but as children, what did they know?

My grandmother spoke Spanish, and in English, she had an accent and spoke in slang. We'd get into a riot of laughter when she'd joke and try to say a curse word, "Bish." She'd love to joke with names like "Lola" for a street worker, and the way she dragged her, "L," was hilarious, or she'd say, "Chit." My grandmother was cute, and when she smiled, her entire face lit up.

I recall a time when my brother went to visit Grandma, and he had a beer in his hand. My grandmother was a dedicated Christian who kept a large Bible as big as her coffee table opened up in her living room. My mother walked in and saw my brother drinking his brew as he talked and visited Grandma. My mom immediately scolds my brother for bringing a beer into my grandma's house. My grandmother, in response, scolded my mother, saying, "This is my house; this is my grandson. He is not hurting anyone, and we are having a nice visit. Leave him alone. It's ok, drink your beer."

My mother kept silent again, learning about the humble, gentle love & acceptance of her mother. I asked grandmother if I could videotape her, giving us a verbal family heritage and about what life was like for her & grandfather.

I learned that day that my family is rooted in

Royalty, as her parents were wealthy. Each morning, Grandmother would be awoken by her mother to assist in their morning routine of preparing meals. My grandmother's mom would wake her early in the morning and tell her to "get up; we have to go feed the people who are walking by and are hungry."

My grandmother would assist her mother in preparing food for the townspeople and farm workers who were paid to work their farmlands. They'd prepare homemade meals in large pots and homemade tortillas to fill and make burritos to feed the people as they walked past.

That's how my grandmother met my grandfather. They were just kids with big dreams of escaping to the promised land, "A land of opportunity," in her words, to start their own family and gain a fresh new beginning. It must have been dreamy as they'd speak from their hearts of what life could be like in this faraway land.

They'd made their dreams a reality and succeeded in a time of poverty and struggles.

What an incredible insight for such young individuals, and how brave they must have been to leave everything familiar to them and not look back.

What a great accomplishment! My grandmother was a true patriot who loved this country. She paid her taxes and Church tithes even when she could no longer attend church services due to her aging body. Our pastor used to visit my grandmother regularly to deliver sermons so she didn't miss out on the messages.

We'd jokingly ask grandmother if grandfather kidnapped her as he was older than her, and she'd laugh and say, "You can't kidnap the willing."

I truly had great examples in my life emulating the heart of Christ, and for this, I am thankful.

"I will make you into a Great Nation, and I will Bless you."

~Genesis 12:2

Then the Lord said to Abraham, "Leave your country, your kindred, and your father's household, and go to the land I will show you. I will make you into a great Nation."

Chapter 9

SEARCHING FOR TRUTHS

"Then You Shall know the truth, and the truth Shall set you free."

~John 8:32

I have reverence for truth, but I do not know what truth is; I suspect there are many truths, and therefore, I suspect all who claim to have the truth.

During and after my divorce, I became desperate to seek Truth, the meanings of life, and spirituality. I longed for true wisdom, knowledge, and understanding.

The Greek word for TRUTH is Aletheia, which refers to "Divine Revelation" and is related to a word that literally means "What Can't be Hidden." I was in search of that hidden truth.

I'd moved to the south part of Sacramento to be closer to the hospital I worked for. Therefore, every day, I passed by a shop with a flashing sign that read, "Psychic Readings." One day, I saw that flashing sign and thought, "What could this hurt?" as I became curious. I lost my direction, and therefore, I disregarded God and my instincts, which clearly taught me to trust Him alone.

I ventured into the shop and was met by a youthful, pretty lady with a soft voice. I thought, "How could this be so bad?" The shop was so intriguing that I couldn't help but want to learn more about it. I was consoling myself, wondering how this could be wrong. I explained things away and compromised with an uncompromising God.

The Young Lady asked me to kindly take a seat in a tiny room in the back of the shop. There was a small round table next to a window tucked into one corner, with her on one side and me on the other. On top of the table were a Crystal ball, a deck of cards, and a few crystals here and there.

As this lady sat before me, staring into a Crystal Ball, she directed me to shuffle the cards and lay them back down. I did as I was told, and she spread them out across the table and told me to pick a few and lay them face up. I did exactly what she instructed me to do, and then she began the "Reading."

Every single card reads, "Soul Mate." She explained to me that I was destined to be with and build a life with my "Soul mate." She read into the Crystal Ball about a long, loving, happy life with my mate. She then instructed me to choose a pure white candle from a glass case and to light it in order to bring clarity to my life. What happened next was *Pure Chaos* as everything in my life turned upside down.

The loving man I was dating suddenly became distant and cold. A series of issues started cropping up one after another. God was sending me clear warnings that what I was doing was unacceptable, but I failed to obey. Then, one day, I came out of my home to find a dead animal on my porch.

Still, I failed to recognize that anything involving death, especially of an innocent animal, was a clear sign to "back out." My neighbor kindly came over to safely get rid of the carcass, and I tried to put it out of my mind.

I was then invited to this psychic woman's house. As I pulled up to the driveway, I noticed a lady pacing on their porch back and forth as though in a trance and then quietly taking a seat in a patio chair. It seemed like she was not in her right mind, as she appeared to be detached from reality.

Sara, "The Fortune Teller," told me to pay her no mind. She then began to tell me all about the lady's history. She was a client of her mother-in-law, who would come to her for "readings."

This Lady once had a very loving family, a great marriage, and a successful career. She came to her mother-in-law, who was a "fortune Teller," and then tragedy struck. The Lady lost her job, her husband, and loving family members, and then she lost her mind.

She then said, "She's like our cat. This lady wanders over to our house, sits on the porch sometimes, all day long, and then wanders back home. This is her daily routine. Sometimes, we feed her. She sits here because she wants to see my Mother-in-law. I don't know what she wants or is waiting for, but that's what she does, and we are too kind to chase her away. So we allow her to stay."

This struck me as odd and bizarre because the

lady appeared lost as a wandering, empty shell of a person with no soul and no life of her own. This was a red flag warning.

Later, I was invited by this fortune teller, Sara, to an event in which she would "renew her vows and therefore earn a higher Ranking" in her practiced religion. She stated that this was her "promotion," much like a graduating Ceremony.

All the leaders from her covenant would be present for this evening's ceremony, and she was giving me a VIP invitation to join them. As I stood outside with her, listening to her excitement and in my mind being reminded of the "Cat Lady," God began to speak very clearly to me. He commanded me, "Don't you dare go!" God warned me that "You will be their Sacrifice."

He then said, "You seen that Cat Lady? That will be you!"

I listened to God's voice, and that day, I left my "psychic" friend behind and never looked back. I was treading on dangerous waters unknown without a paddle, and God's graces and mercies followed me, warning me of the dangers ahead.

I was wise enough to heed His warning and turn back around safely to shore. How many times has God spoken to your heart, warning you of the dangers ahead? Did you heed His warnings and turn your direction towards the Cross?

God says in His word, "I will never leave you nor forsake you,"

~Deuteronomy 3:18

And in my life, I've found this to be true.

This was eleven years ago, and to this day, I still have no soul mate. In fact, I have been quite unfortunate in "Love." Therefore, I have not dated in a very long time.

For many years, I reasoned that if, in fact, I have gifts of prophecy, how could this be any different? We prophesy in the church, so how was this type of psychic gift any different, and how was it so wrong to seek assistance and direction from another prophet in my life?

What I hadn't considered asking myself was, is this from God? What is the source of prophecy in which I chose to seek, believe, and therefore trust and, in turn, praise a foreign God, for God says, *"We shall have no other Gods before Him!"* (Exodus 20: 3-5) or any likeness of anything that is in Heaven above.

Anything not of God is against God, but I was too self-serving to admit it. I got "hooked" on the readings and was highly gifted in the spiritual; I felt it tenfold.

I got hooked on the "High" it gave me, as the Bible Says,

"for Satan himself transforms himself into an angel of light."

~2 Corinthians 11:14

I began to see and hear spirits, and my prophetic gifts were heightened, but I was not walking in pure truth, as I had one foot in and one foot out. I was cheating! What spilled out of me was not of God, and I knew it and felt it!

It is one thing to trample on the gates of hell but

to trample on a much more powerful source, which is the kingdom of heaven and the source of all powers, is a dangerous feat! Out of the blue, I would be overcome with feelings of panic and a sense of worthlessness. It was very difficult to shake, and I began to sleep with the lights on.

I'd hear my doorbell ring with nobody there, and I'd hear knocks on the walls. My bed would shake vigorously, jarring me awake, heart pounding rapidly. I'd see people who'd recently passed before it was made known to the public, and I'd see how they died, and I knew things about people before they'd tell me.

I believe these were what the Bible speaks about, "Unclean" spirits. What does the living have to do with the dead? It drained me, and I had a difficult time sleeping. I didn't know what these spirits wanted from me & I didn't want to find out!!

One night, as I slept, I was suddenly jarred out of my sleep, and what stood before me was a young girl in distress: She was soaking wet & had long, blonde hair. I saw that she had gone off a short body of land and into a steep body of water in her vehicle not far from where she was originally parked. As she stood before me, clothes draping her body, I was then jarred fully awake, and I screamed so loudly that I awoke the others in my house. I explained what I'd seen & later we found out that a young girl not far from where I lived had actually been found drowned in her car who looked exactly like the girl who appeared before me that night.

I was too afraid to ask, "What do you want?" I now pray for her family and loved ones, and I pray she rests in peace. So much is unknown about the spirit world, but I do know that if God needed my help, he'd have let me know!

Why God would trust mankind with His truths- is beyond my understanding. But I do know this: I do not want to be outside of God's will. I'd rather work for God than against Him because I could never win in this life or the next without the help of God on my side. God is the creator of all things great and small, who knows me better than I know myself. He created me, and because of this, I want no counterfeit in my life.

One Day, I realized this and cried out to God, "Lord, I cannot shake this addiction, and I know this is not your Will for me as it goes against your Truths! If I am to be free from his bondage, I need your help!"

I'd been sleeping one evening, and it was dark in my room as I overcame my fear and turned down the lights. Suddenly, in a panic, I was pinned to my bed by a humongous creature approximately the size of my room who appeared as a skeletal, powerful entity, and I knew it could literally kill me. I was stuck in a paralytic state as it pierced at me with glaring eyes that literally struck me with pure panic. I couldn't move, and I could barely breathe as it hovered over me with its claws embedded into the flesh of my wrists. It demanded, "Who will you serve?" I couldn't speak, but by the third command, I was able to force out the word, "JESUS!" It released me and then vanished. I awoke gasping for air, and strangely, I was left with scratches on my wrists in reality. I knew then that I had to make a choice, or my life could literally be taken from me.

I found myself on my knees in repentance, and as I did, I felt the need to puke my guts out! Something from deep down inside of me, from the depths of my being and out of my guts, a sort of wrenching feeling, and out of my mouth forcefully pulling and jerking me in anguish. It came up and out and then continued for hours and days as God called me to fast and pray.

Just when I thought it was over, I'd be on my face again, pouring out a Gut-wrenching cry to God with such force that I knew I was being delivered. Exhausted and depleted, I knew God was restoring me and cleansing me from all that was not of Him. He was healing me from my anguish and from years of Spiritual abuse.

I was a believer in God & of Christ as Savior, knowing the truth, and in this truth, I knew that I was being delivered from these demonization spirits that had attempted to influence and rule my life. In my surrender, I felt the freedom as my soul was lifted from the heaviness of this oppression I had endured for the past decade.

I fully Surrendered, allowing God to cleanse me from every unclean thing that had threatened my life. I began to fall in love with the World of God, and now, for the first time in my life, they had true meaning. I thought I knew God, and I thought because I could quote scripture that I'd mastered it, but I was wrong. When you finally know, you know, and when we really know better, we do better, as this was the situation with me, in my experiences, in my life.

It felt like a vault of True wisdom and understanding had been replaced as my vessel was poured out before God; he poured into me a renewed understanding of His Truth & His Position in my life.

And I thanked Him for Loving me so much that He would meet me where I was in all of my filth, set me free, and deliver me of my uncleanliness!

I fell in love with God & prayed with all my heart, asking for forgiveness. I actually felt saved, and it is truly invigorating!

I threw out every Candle or Crystal I had collected and replaced them with Bibles. I slept so well for the first time in years, and I felt God's love surround me like a baby in the womb. My slumber was sweet, and I found my way back home.

"When you lie down, you will not be afraid; when you lie down, your sleep will be sweet."

~ Proverbs 3:24

Although I knew that what I was doing Was wrong and displeasing to God, as one cannot serve God and Satan, you are either on one side or the other. I believe God allowed these experiences to open my eyes to The Spiritual Realms, both dark and light, expanding my understanding. I learned that darkness, although it may present itself as light, is far from it. It is powerful and nothing to fool with, as some of the things I experience require a sacrifice in exchange. Something had to give, as nothing but salvation is free. In the end, one may lose something extremely vital, such as One's Sanity.

I learned that we cannot purposely bend God's will for Our Own favor, as there are always consequences to pay, and these consequences are not worth losing God's favor.

I brought on spirits upon myself that did not feel good, accompanied by pure dread. I literally heard them Calling my name, and things literally flew off my dressers and shelves, crashing onto the floor as they did not want to let me go.

I did not like the things I experienced. Once I fully surrendered to God, turned away from these magical arts, pleaded forgiveness, & received deliverance, it all went away. The harassment, dread, and oppression are all gone. In place of it came Peace & Rest. I choose to believe in the goodness of God. Only God gives us a Spirit of Power, love, and a Sound mind. (Bible)

If you are stuck in despair, trust God, give it to him, and experience His peace. Only He can fully supply our needs.

I've Wandered Far Away From God

I've wandered far away from God,

Now I'm Coming home;

The Paths of sin too long I've tried,

Lord, I'm coming home.

I've wasted many precious years.

Now, I'm coming home.

I now repent with bitter tears.

Lord, I'm coming home...

Chapter 10

ADVENTURES AND MEMORIALS BEYOND THE VEIL

During this period, on my mission to understand truth, I found myself traveling out into nature. I encountered the most beautiful scenarios: sunsets, lakes, mountains, ocean beaches, and animal nature.

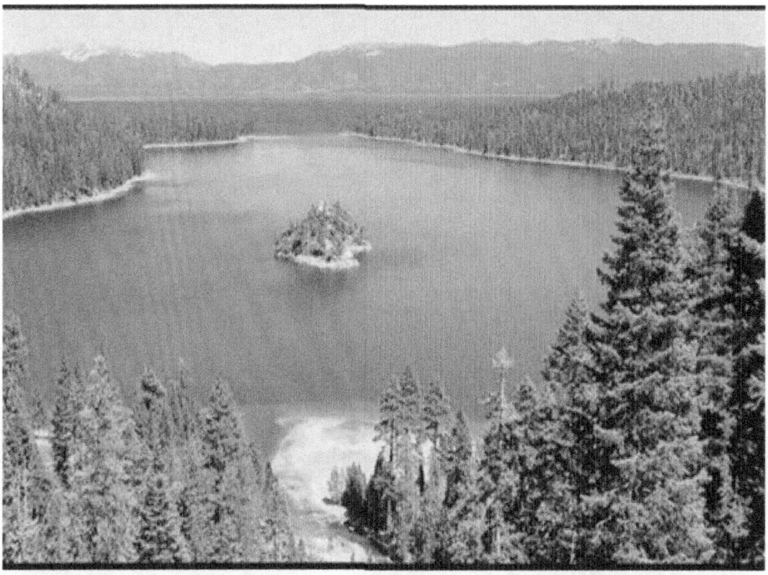

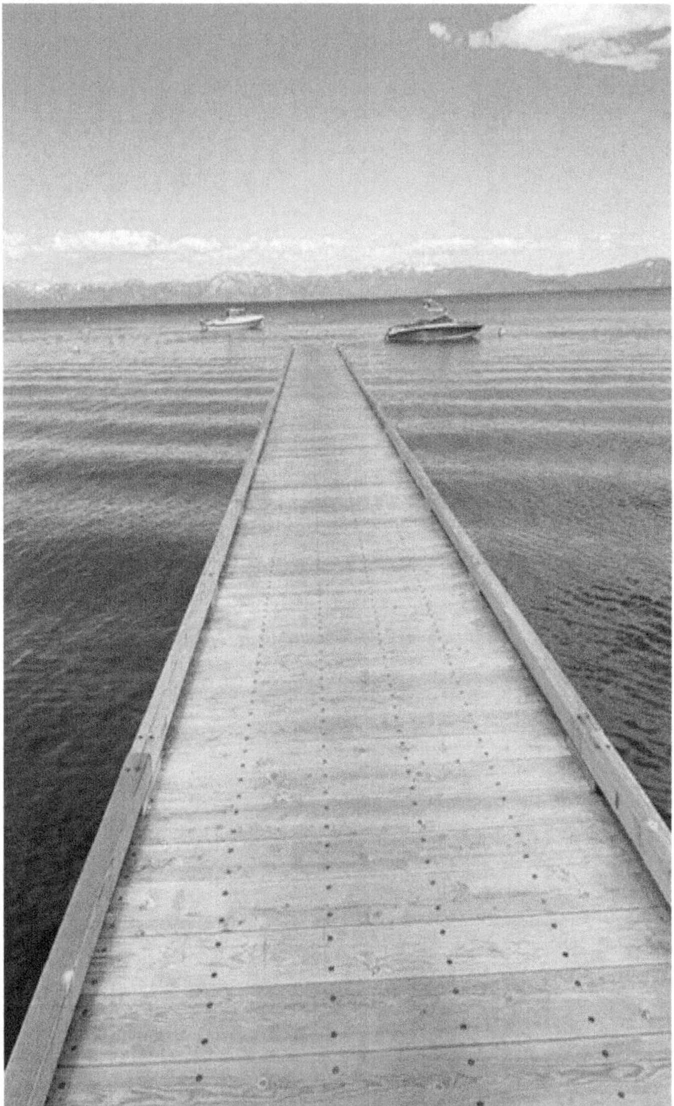

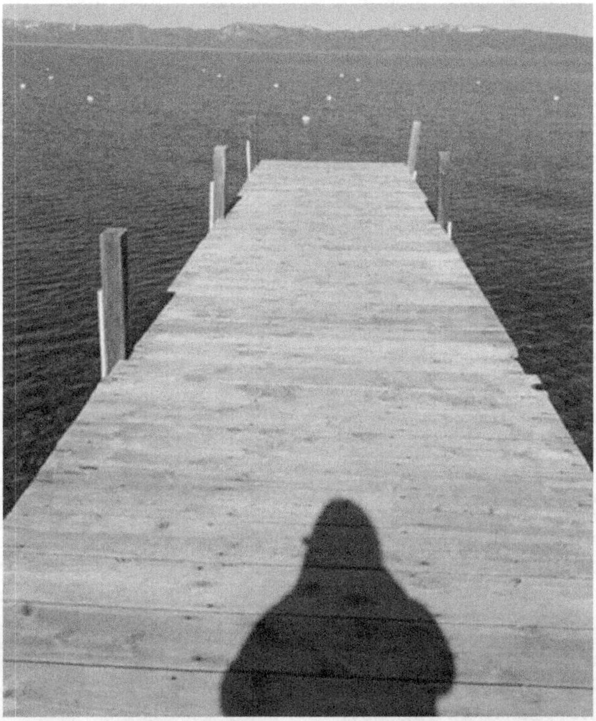

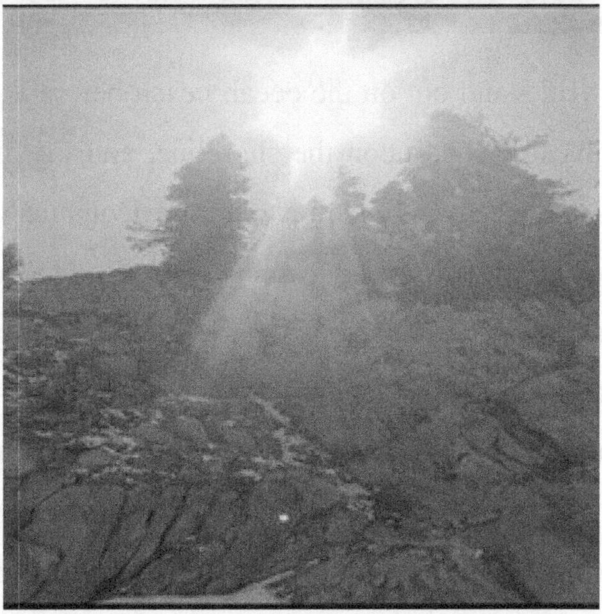

I'd stand out on the ocean beach before Sunrise as Waves crashed upon the shoreline, and I'd lift my hands to the heavens and pray out loud. Dolphins would appear in the distance, leaping from the water and making splashes along the ocean's edge. Butterflies would land on my hands, deer would appear in the mountains, and a dove might show up out of nowhere. I began to capture it all on camera, and on one of these adventures, as the sun was setting, my camera lost its cells, and the screen went black. I kept snapping, adamant about getting every last photo I could get as the Sun shone brilliantly and miraculously beautiful that day. When I got home and recharged the battery to take a look at all my photos, a beautiful transparent apparition with Angelic faces was shown in a photo. I know now that God, in His infinite Glory, approved of my decision to trust Him and, therefore, validated that I was now on the right track!

I ventured up to Lake Tahoe and drove up and around glorious mountainsides. I came upon rows of piers at the lake's dock and found the one without locked gates around it.

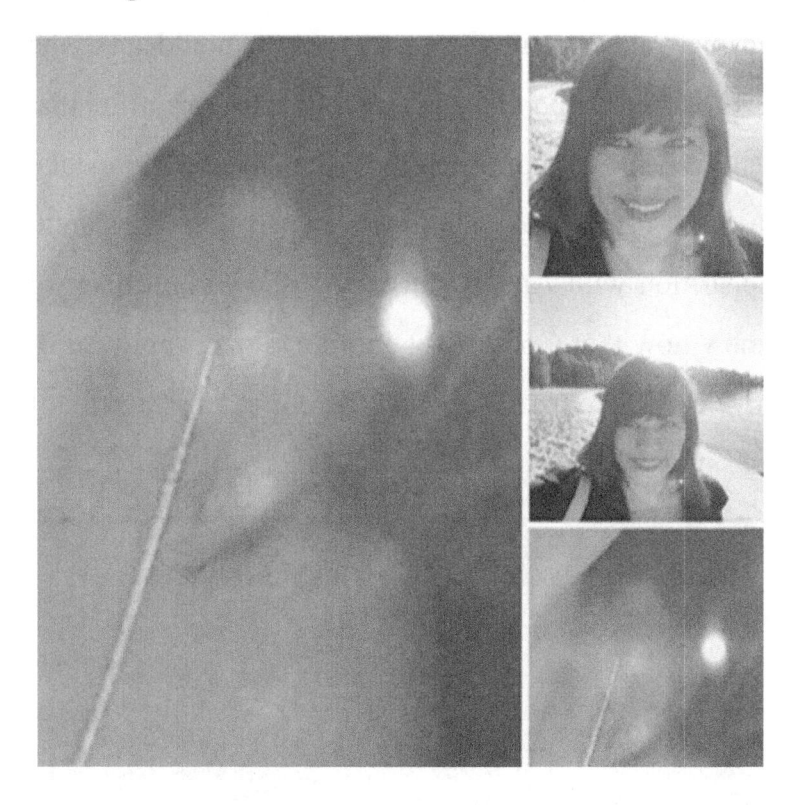

I walked to the edge, taking in the scenery, amazed at how the waters sparkled like diamonds and breathing in the pine scent from the trees surrounding the lake.

I knelt down and carved in my sister & brother's names, who'd died much too soon, and also my precious baby girl's name. I made a memorial right there in that place.

I'd driven far around this mountain, not knowing where it would take me, and parked on the side of a busy highway. My sister's name, Elizabeth, was left carved in that wooden spot on that pier along with my brother and my baby, and I felt satisfied as I said a prayer, knowing I'd have a beautiful place to return to in remembrance of them.

When I left that place, I knew I'd have to turn around to avoid going further up into this mountain. The only turning point was a way up, as the road was narrow with blind spots and oncoming traffic.

As I found the spot to turn around on the first street up ahead, my eyes were set on the sign on the edge of the street.

I gasped to my utter amazement, not believing what I was staring at. Right there in front of me was a street sign that read, "ELIZABETH WAY." My sister's name was in Bold Capital Letters! I knew that- I knew that- I knew that; I was being led as all of this was no mere coincidence!

I cried all the way on the drive back down that mountain, wiping away the flood of tears pouring down my face, clouding my view of the road ahead.

I was amazed at God and perplexed by how

much He cared for a heart like mine—a seemingly insignificant person seeking healing and trying to find my small space in this vast world of thousands upon thousands and billions of His great creations.

How is it that I mattered so much to Him that He'd care about these things that mattered so much to me?

I marveled and poured out my heart in thankfulness to God, My father, who sticks closer than a friend.

He cares about the things that matter most to me, so I can trust Him with my life and with all my Futures.

Proverbs 18:24,

"A man that hath friends must shew himself friendly: and there is a friend that sticketh closer than a brother."

That friend is Jesus Christ. He is the Lord of our lives and our Savior.

Are you a friend of God?

During nursing school, we would choose groups

for our clinicals, and it was during this time that I met my friend, Tasha. We were coupled together for our rotations, and at that time, she wasn't married. We would talk about our goals and dreams.

She'd talk about her dreams of marrying the love of her life, and now she wanted a family of her own and children. She'd struggled for some time in nursing school, and I'd encourage her by telling her that "Quitting is not an option," so we stuck it out and got through it together.

Afterward, we both accepted a position at the hospital where I still work as a registered nurse. Tasha had excelled and earned herself a "Daisy Award," which is such a great accomplishment for her, especially considering that one of our clinical instructors once told her that she'd "never make it as a RN." This remark weighed heavily on her, and she often shared her doubts with me when we met.

Tasha earned herself a plaque on the wall down one of the busy corridors in the hospital, which is visible to all.

She'd accomplished her goals and married a nice young man, and together, they had three adorable children. One evening, Tasha was not feeling well, as she'd been on a fast with her church, where she played the piano. She thought it was due to being exhausted from work and the fast, so she asked her husband to watch the children while she took a short nap.

Her husband later went to check on her and couldn't wake her up, so they rushed her to our hospital, where attempts were made to revive her without success.

It was later revealed that during this fast, her blood sugars dropped so low, slipping her into a coma in which the doctors couldn't find any pulse. She was laid to rest with our coworkers at her side.

I couldn't bring myself to attend as I took her death very hard because I knew what a great person she was and how she longed for the life she lived. She'd struggled and worked hard to accomplish all her goals and succeeded in fulfilling every one of them.

Tasha had a heart for this world, and that's what

she fasted for to bring salvation to the lost people & peace to a dying world! She'd died on her young child's birthday, and I was deeply saddened for her family. I struggled to understand such tragedy in the face of the goodness of God.

One night soon after, I lay next to my boyfriend, who I thought would become my husband one day. I was in deep sleep when suddenly, my friend Tasha stood before me with her arms reaching out to me.

I couldn't see her face, as she was all lit up like a bright light bulb, her hands glowing like glow sticks and illuminating the purest love and joy. I knew her without having to see her face, and I felt her love and joy as she reached out to me. I communicated to her that she was not supposed to be here as I backed away, then awoke gasping desperately for air and to take a breath.

It shook my boyfriend awake & I told him what I'd just experienced. It was morning, and I'd been dealing with my own health issues and was under my doctor's care. My blood levels had dropped dangerously low, prompting recent blood work. I wasn't feeling well, so I contacted my doctor and found out that my blood sugar levels were in the 40s. As a result of my blood work, my hemoglobin had dropped to 6 and was continuing to fall. I was called in for emergency admission & surgery. It was a close call, but I am now back in good health. It was a scary time in my life.

I believe my friend Tasha took that opportunity to support me and to communicate to me that she is happy and still alive & able to help even from beyond the veil.

I choose to believe in the afterlife, and I choose to believe a glorious life full of love and joy awaits us on the other side, more realistic than what we experience here on this earth. It is our reward for living a wholesome and good life caring for others.

Every brush I have had with death, I have repeated to my lord, "I'm not ready yet."

When my precious daughter passed before touching this earth, I was left to grieve. On one occasion, I was washing dishes and looking out the window in deep thought when all of a sudden, I'd get a warm sensation come over me, and my nostrils would be overcome with a fragment scent of flowers like a lovely perfume. It would flood the air around me and linger for a while. Then, one day, it was gone, and I was left with the memories of a trauma that I'd endured to try to make sense of it in a world that kept moving on without mercy for a grieving soul.

Song of Solomon 2:1-3,

"I am the rose of Sharon and the lily of the valleys. As the lily among thorns, so is my love among the daughters." *As the apple tree among the trees of the wood, so is my beloved among the sons. I sat down under his shadow with great delight, and his fruit was sweet to my taste."*

I've encountered many people in my career as a healthcare professional who have claimed to have near-death experiences. Every one of them has confessed it brought about significant life changes.

One man who we found pulseless and we'd revived came out of it claiming; I saw Jesus!" The Doctor asked, "Who did you see?" The man excitedly said, "Jesus!" I have seen Jesus."

As I took care of one gentleman at the end of his life, his spouse was struggling with some very difficult and deep emotions. She could not understand how or why such a well-known, accomplished, and delightful man could be dying of this dreadful disease. She was quite upset & found it difficult to come to terms with it all.

As she spoke at the bedside, I allowed her the space to express herself in a productive and therapeutic way. All of a sudden, this man started frantically motioning to his wife. He quickly wrote something down on his tablet, as he could no longer speak.

She read the note, looked surprised, and then looked over at me. He motioned for her to read his note to me. She slowly read the note, which said, "When you two were talking over there, a huge Angel appeared next to the nurse and was leaned over whispering into her ear."

I knew I'd felt a flood of peace wash over me, and as I spoke with his Spouse, the right words came rolling off my tongue. I'm always grateful for Divine angelic intervention.

Psalms 91:11-12,

"For he shall give his angels charge over thee, to keep thee in all thy ways. They shall bear thee up in their hands, lest thou dash thy foot against a stone."

When My grandmother was hospitalized for the last time, we all took turns to visit her at her bedside. She'd caught a respiratory infection, and it was not shaking. She'd grown weak and lost her appetite. We were all informed to visit her and prepare for our final "Goodbyes."

Then, when my turn came, and as I spoke with my grandmother, I asked her to take care of my daughter for me until I joined them one day.

Grandmother nodded her head in agreement, folded her hands around mine, and she wouldn't let go. She started giving me her blessings. I was caught up in the moment, not knowing what to do. I was so overwhelmed with emotions that I started to cry. The family that had gathered in the room panicked and ushered me out. Still, Grandmother did not want to let go. We had connected on a higher, deeper level, and so she gave her blessings, which I am grateful to receive. I took those blessings to heart, praying for our family, and I haven't stopped since. My grandmother understood the dynamics of losing a child and, in her final hours, wanted me to know this. She wanted to comfort me and offer her blessings. I readily received it.

I have asked the same questions throughout my life that you are probably contemplating right now. Why me? Why Would God allow someone like me to experience so many seemingly miraculous, mysterious, unexplainable, and spiritual encounters? Perhaps the only reasonable explanation is that I have been open to receiving. God is all I've had at times to turn to, and He knew I'd write about it and share it with you, the One reading this right now.

God wants you to know that He is an Unchanging, unwavering, Miracle-Working, resurrecting God. If you would only put your Trust in Him, you would encounter the same and even better life-changing encounters.

He tells us in John 14:12,

"Verily, verily, I say unto you, He that believeth

on me, the works that I do shall he do also; and greater works than these shall he do; because I go unto my Father."

You are reading this now because God wants you to know this.

Chapter 11

I'M GOING HOME

Many times in my childhood,
When we'd traveled so far by nightfall,
How weary I'd grown.
Father's arms would slip around me, and gently, he'd say,
My child, we're going home.
Going home, I'm going home.
There is nothing to hold me here.
I've caught a glimpse of that heavenly land,
Praise God, I'm going home.

I was 11 years old when my sister Anita walked up to me and said, "I know something you don't know. It is a secret: Your Dad is not your Real Dad- you have a whole other Dad."

I replied, "So what! I already know." She warned, "You better not tell anyone that I told you."

I kept the oath not to reveal our secret, knowing that both she and I were aware of my mysterious Dad out there, who probably had no idea that I even existed. I looked at my small face in the mirror and wondered, "Do I look like him? If I do, then which part of me resembles him?" Then, I began to guess what he might look like.

I'd wondered if I passed him in public places, questioning if every man who carried his name could possibly be my biological Dad. I started looking at men in public who were around my mother's age and who may share similar features, wondering, "Are you my Dad?"

I'd fantasize about meeting him and introducing him to the daughter he never knew he had. I imagined us hanging out together, him spoiling me. There were so many things I wanted to know and wanted him to know about me and my life. I wanted him to know that I played the clarinet, made the basketball team, and was on the Honor roll. I was a really good kid on the cheer team and excelled in Math, English & Science. I loved to read a good book. I wanted to hear all about his life and find out if I have siblings.

Through the years, as time moved on, I searched

for him. I went to County Records, but with just a name, it was difficult to track a person down. I heard a rumor that he was killed after winning lots of money at a game of poker, but later found out this was false news.

I sought help from a detective, but with limited information available, I eventually gave up any hopes of ever knowing his identity. I convinced myself that it was okay not to know and that perhaps there was a reason for it. Yet, it still haunted me- the not knowing, so it kept me in wonder.

Through experience, I learned about the consequences of overcorrection. One day, my sister took me along to babysit our neighbor's kids—a girl and two boys who were older than me.

The boys thought it would be fun to try to "fly" like Superman. So, we stacked plastic crates on top of each other until we had a tall tower, forming a makeshift platform on which to stand and jump.

There were T-shaped concrete metal poles at opposite ends of an outdoor clothesline. We aimed to jump from the crates, catch them with our hands, swing them, and then fly into the air and land on our feet.

I waited patiently for my turn as each boy took their leap and soared through the air. When my turn came, I was determined to literally fly just like they had.

With the boys counting down, "One, two, three & Jump!!!"

As my little legs climbed up and steadied themselves, I eyed the pole while the boys counted down. In my mind, I said, "Ready, Set, Go!" and I jumped, arms outstretched like Superman. For a moment, I did fly, but then I felt a thump as my belly hit the hard dirt, and my face landed face down. My arms were still spread out, and I felt the pain as I busted my nose and lips, blood pouring onto the ground and onto my face.

The boys gasped in horror as I finally got up from the ground and ran toward the fence. I climbed over the crunched-in metal and dashed through the alley, holding my little face covered in blood, screaming all the way home. I vaulted over another small fence, raced through our backyard, and burst through our back door, where I found Mom in the kitchen- cooking dinner.

One look at me, bloody and crying in agony, and Mom dropped everything to hold me in her arms. Once she knew I was safe and could get me to speak, all she heard were the boys' names. With a wet cloth on my face, she demanded, "Who did this?" With me in Tow, Mom marched down the alley to their house. The boys hid, and my sister got an earful of Mom's wrath. After my Mom calmed down enough, she gathered information from the boys and me about what happened. From then on, I was not allowed to play with those boys or accompany my sister while she babysat.

Through this experience, I felt my mother's protective love, much like God's love for us. I also learned the consequences of overcorrecting, overthinking, and trying to defy gravity in a way my body was not designed for.

Therefore, as a remembrance of this incident, I decided not to force God's hand in attempting to track down my biological father, who was absent from my life. Why attempt to bend reality? If he truly wanted to be found, then that opportunity would have presented itself without forcing me to jump from insecure and unstable heights to secure my spot! Therefore, I left it alone.

Later in my adult life, as I sat in my dentist's chair after taking my annual X-rays, he turned to me and asked, "Did you ever have any injury to your face as a child, particularly to your teeth? One of your teeth shows a dead root right here in the front." I thought back to that day and replied, "Yes, Doctor, I did, in fact; what do you see?" The dentist explained that I had a completely dead nerve in my right front tooth that traveled up toward my nasal cavity.

I giggled to myself and shook my head, recalling that "Free-flying feeling." As a child, I literally defied gravity and actually flew through the air, arms stretched up and out. I didn't have a cape, nor was I a superhero, but for a brief moment, I felt like one—until I nose-dived and 'Bit the Dust.'

Needless to say, because of the discoloration of a dead nerve to a dead tooth, I had it repaired, and now I have a bright, white smile that I take advantage of showing every chance I get because I have truly earned it!

There was also a great surprise and reward in store for me, as the powers that be understood the longing in a young girl's heart to simply find her place in this world. It was in letting go, scars and all, that my path unfolded before me.

Through this, I discovered that the greatest strength lies in releasing situations that feel too burdensome for my shoulders to bear. In letting go, I learned to trust that everything meant for me will naturally come together in due time.

Isaiah 49:15 says,

"I will not forget you. Behold, I have engraved you on the palms of my hands; your walls are continually before me."

Deuteronomy 31:8 says:

"It is the Lord who goes before you. He will be with you; he will not leave you or forsake you. Do not fear or be dismayed."

God will become your parent, your helper, and

your protector! Amen.

Chapter 12

MUSIC; THIS IS MY SONG

Listening to or playing music provides a total brain workout. It has been known to keep our brains intact throughout the aging process. It provides a way for us to express our feelings with or without words. It pulls on our heartstrings and allows us to make sense of our lives. It increases blood flow to brain regions that generate and control emotions.

According to Pfizer, our limbic system "lights up" when our ears perceive music.

Limbic System: *It is involved in processing emotions and controlling memory.*

Humans' understanding of music is intuitive. It can evoke strong emotions in listeners, and even animals respond to music. Music can be a source of comfort, joy, and inspiration, and it is inherently social, bringing people together.

Music improves our quality of life. It also has the

power to uplift one's mood by triggering dopamine release in our brains. Dopamine is our feel-good hormone, which activates our brain's pleasure and reward system.

God gives us music to bring us joy and delight. It is a gift that helps us to grasp His love and the knowledge of salvation. Jesus and His disciples often sang Psalms, which are songs of Praise.

Dancing is also a common musical expression.

In the Bible, Psalms 149:3 says,

"Let them praise his name with dancing and make music to him with timbrel and harp."

In Samuel 6:14-22,

"Wearing a linen ephod, David was dancing before the Lord with all his might."

David dances before the Lord with all of his might, providing us with a wonderful example of the true meaning of total surrender to God in Worship.

Psalms 149: 3-5,

"Let them praise his name with dancing and

make music to him with timbrel and harp. For the Lord takes delight in his people; he crowns the humble with victory. Let his faithful people rejoice in this honor and sing for joy on their beds."

It is a sacred dance offered in worship that is acceptable and pleasing to God.

Zephaniah 3:17

"The Lord your God is with you, the Mighty Warrior who saves. He will take great delight in you; in his love, he will no longer rebuke you but will rejoice over you with singing."

He will dance with you, shouting joy for you. Our dance can become our prayer, allowing both physical and spiritual expression.

I have played several instruments, including flute, clarinet, guitar, piano, and congos, without mastering this art; however, I have learned that tune or melody is the most important. If you have ever heard a guitar riff or catchy bass line, you have also experienced that strong instrument hook—this is a melody.

In the note, a melody with the right rhythm

played in harmony becomes the three basic elements of music. Then, we can understand the heart and soul of music.

Our own music and heart songs are meant to draw our hearts and attention to God's glory, His power, and His love. It deepens our love for God in innumerable ways as we pour our hearts out to Him and encounter His gifts.

In your unique dance and song of worship to God, we have a purpose to bring healing, peace, inspiration, and encouragement.

God has put a special song in your heart. It exists in order to celebrate all that is worthy in which your soul delights. In this, you invite and welcome God's supernatural presence to manifest the desires and passion in your heart.

Psalms 22:3 states,

"But thou art holy, O thou that inhabitest the praises of Israel."

This verse speaks directly to the idea that God's presence inhabits the praises of His people, and where

His presence is, there's fullness of joy. We can worship God even in our distress.

In my profession, as a nurse, I get the opportunity to work with an aging population. Many lose the capacity to communicate clearly. Then, I found a unique way to connect with some by asking about their favorite songs. I'd find the song on YouTube or over the internet and play it for them. Can you believe that many people sing every word with emotions as their minds trace back to the days in their past when they converse about their treasured memories of days gone by? I find it fascinating how our brains connect with our hearts through music to bring up an array of emotions relevant to our past memories, invoking one to engage with clarity through conversation.

This is a powerful example of how deeply music connects people and our society.

I read a very cool poem by an unknown author that reflects how music is truly a universal language.

Reflections of a Boomer

I've seen fire, and I've seen rain.

I've been through the desert on a horse with no name.

I've gone to Kansas City, and I sang in the sunshine.

I've been on the road again with Georgia on my mind.

Like a rolling stone, I've given peace a chance.

I've put a camel to bed and danced the last dance.

Mr. Tambourine man played a song for me,

I've whispered words of wisdom; let it be.

I've fallen into a burning ring of fire and walked the line,

To all the girls I've loved before, you were always on my mind.

I've been everywhere; I've been so lonesome I could cry,

I've driven my Chevy to the levee when the levee was dry.

I've been to Itchy Coo Park in a yellow submarine.

I've made the scene in a time machine.

I've done the Hokey Pokey and turned myself around.

I've welcomed the baby back to the poor side of town.

I've followed the tracks of my tears down a long and winding road.

I've kept on searching, for a heart of gold.

I've sought shelter from the storm; I've sat on the dock

of the bay.

I've rocked around the clock on a sunshiny day.

I've knocked on Heaven's door while blowing in the wind.

Joy to the world, those were the days, my friend.

Lay lady lay in crimson and clover.

It's been a hard day's night, and now the party's over.

Psalms 150:1-6

"Praise the Lord. Praise God in his sanctuary; praise him in his mighty heavens. Praise him for his acts of power; praise him for his surpassing greatness. Praise him with the sounding of the trumpet, praise him with the harp and lyre, Praise him with timbrel and dancing. Praise him with the strings and pipe, Praise him with the clash of cymbals, praise him with resounding cymbals. Let everything that has breath praise the Lord. Praise the Lord."

Chapter 13

THE ART & BEAUTY OF SURRENDER

"No memory is ever alone; it's at the end of a trail of memories, a dozen trails that each have their own associations."

~Louis L'Amour

COMING HOME:

It was a regular day at work, and my coworker gave me a report. I was told about an elderly person who had some depression and was refusing medications. The patient was confused and unable to follow directions. There were medications to help with these symptoms, but the patient refused to take them; therefore, we could hear the patient calling out from the room in distress.

As I made my rounds and walked into the room, I suddenly stopped in my tracks. I said, "*Tio?*" which is an endearment in Spanish that translates to "Uncle."

He looked at me through teary eyes and called out my name. I asked, "You remember me?" As I had not seen this family member since childhood. Time and distance had kept us apart.

He said, "Yes, little Tina!"

From that moment, tears of joy flowed freely. We talked about past memories and about our family. We cried and laughed together. I asked, "Will you please take your medicine?" He agreed, "Yes." And from that point on, he began to heal.

I've come to realize in my profession of healing that there is a place deep inside of our heart space that recognizes our connections through love and this is the place which brings us the highest level of healing.

This soul space is often connected to our higher self, where we experience wholeness.

This is the amazing thing about love and family, especially those that support you in your life. Those bonds are unbreakable even when they no longer exist in the physical. They remain in the memories of your heart.

These connections are powerful in nature. In fact, in my life and profession, I've personally encountered people who, as they approach the end of life, claim to not only see their loved ones but also encounter our Loving Savior Jesus! Their near-death experiences often include vivid, comforting visions of both family and divine presence, which reinforces the deep, spiritual connections that surpass the physical world.

These experiences aren't just hallucinations or dreams but rather as real as this book you now hold in your hands. They see it, feel it with every fiber of their being, and all their senses expand. They experience it with a higher knowledge than in their earthly physical form. They also return with more heightened knowledge than ever before.

How do I know this? I know this because I experienced it myself. I was dying with my daughter when I went to the hospital, seeking and pleading for help. I was experiencing severe pain, and I knew that something was seriously wrong. Even though I was in bad shape, the monitor showed my daughter's heart rhythm. The nurse in my care reported to the Doctor that she "was sending this one home." She believed that I was overreacting and instead requested a muscle relaxant, denying the severity of the situation.

The saddest truth is I was not overreacting, and my daughter unfortunately kicked her little feet for the very last time within my womb. I was blacking out by this time and was hemorrhaging to death. Both my baby and I were in big trouble, but I trusted the healthcare professionals to do what they were trained to do best. Much to their discredit, they missed this time, and my daughter died and nearly took my life, too!

By the time I rushed back to the hospital on my birthday weekend, it was too late, and we got rushed into emergency surgery. My blood pressure was extremely high, and I was septic. I was given boluses of rescue fluid and IV antibiotics. Despite the high fever and blackouts, my baby was delivered. She was beautiful as an angel and perfect in every way, but she was not breathing and had no pulse. The doctor attending me looked dumbfounded and at a loss for words.

I felt myself slipping away and asked God to give me more life as I was not ready to die. I'll keep the rest to myself because it is sacred and holy.

God gave me another chance but told me my suffering on this earth would be great because I had the opportunity to go beyond "The veil," and my trials would be heavier. All I had to do was ask and stay close to God, and He would fight every battle.

I'm here to tell you that God is real, Heaven is real, and you should trust Him with your life.

Yes, my grief was tremendous, and my healing took time, but in all of it, I'm grateful; why? How many people on this earth who are actually living get the opportunity to encounter an angel? I did!

I chose to live and tell my testimony that our lives have purpose and meaning! Even those things we don't fully understand have a purpose and a meaning.

Perhaps we will not gain complete knowledge of it all now, in the moment, nor of God, for that would minimize our purpose and our capacity for growth.

One day, when you have done your very best to walk in your purpose and step into all that God has created you and called you to be to help your fellow man and this entire earth to evolve as you are greatly needed to fulfill God's purpose- not for God's sake but for our sake and your sake.

One day, you will receive your crown of Glory as you stand before the one and only FATHER, God, and He says to you, "Well done, my faithful servant, enter into your rest."

I certainly plan on being there. Won't you?

Back to my story. I've cared for my loved ones in my career and sometimes by accident, but I always welcomed them as they put their trust in me. And I've witnessed miraculous healings. That's the love of family and the power of our souls. It goes way beyond earthly boundaries and connects in a loving realm where the meaning of "AGAPE" is birthed.

I've been so very fortunate to be a part of all of it. God has shown me that I am definitely walking with a purpose. I'd have it no other way.

God defines LOVE: *"Love is patient and kind; Love does not envy or boast; it is not arrogant or rude. It does not insist on its own way; it is not irritable or resentful; it does not rejoice at wrongdoing or resentful;*

it does not rejoice at wrongdoing but rejoices with the truth. Love bears all things, believes all things, hopes all things, endures all things. Love never ends." 1 Corinthians 13:4-8a

It always protects, always trusts, always hopes, always perseveres.

Chapter 14

FINDING OZ

"A good beginning makes a good ending."

~Louis L' Amour

We've all heard of the cliché about there being "light at the end of the tunnel."

I've often wondered what happens when we reach that light, and does it remain the passageway to the promised Manna, as written in the Bible for the Israelites who trusted in and obeyed God without murmuring or complaint?

Is it hardwired within our human nature to naturally experience moments of doubt, especially when life does not unfold as we so desire? Are these the fabrics of learning to trust that "All things eventually work together for good and as they should?"

I sure pray for my faith. Amen!

The interesting thing about surrender is that all that you desire tends to simply "fall" on your lap when you simply "let go."

So, it was in my quest to "find myself" that I desired so desperately to know who I was. That part of me who didn't know the other half.

I believe this is a similar quest for many adopted children, even when we've had a happy home. It feels as though we are walking around with our glass half empty. This is not true, but it "feels" this way.

I'd decided I'd take a DNA test—the one with the swab that you sent through the mail. I thought not much of it. Because what can one truly gain from a swab or from a spit sample? I ordered the one you swab your cheek with, sent it in, and nearly forgot about it. Until weeks later, I received an email with my results.

I didn't open it right away because I didn't take it all that seriously. So, I let it go for a few weeks. When I did open it, I was surprised at the details of the results. It was very interesting. I recovered my percentages and read what each one meant.

I looked through my family heritage links and thought it was incredible that they actually linked me to several of my known family members.

I thought it was coincidental and explained it away with good reasoning.

Surely, I thought there were records validating my family members, so there was nothing surprising about this.

Then, one day, I received an alert that a message from a woman linked to me by DNA was in my mailbox.

Her message read, "Hello, my name is Melissa, and I am very much into genealogy. I've been linked to you with a high DNA match, which makes me curious. Could you tell me more about yourself and your relations so that I may figure out how you match so closely within my family ancestor tree?"

I messaged her back, "Hello, my name is …. And I'm … years old. My D.O.B. is… And I live in … I have a mom named…. And a dad who I do not know. All I have is his name and D.O.B. and where he lived when he dated my mom. I have an idea where his family originated, but that's all I know."

I received a message back. "Ok, now I'm curious. I have a brother with that name, age, and place where he lived before you were born, according to your date of birth. Our DNA links you as a niece, and I'm attempting to figure out how this is possible. The DNA match is so high that I'd like you to take another DNA test, but on this sight where most of our family is registered."

We chatted a bit more, and I informed this kind woman that I'd think about doing this as my heart pounded wildly thinking of the possibilities.

I sat on it for a while as so many thoughts ran through my head. If I decided to do this and I received valid results without a doubt, there would be no turning back. The one secure thing I was informed of is that Melissa was also a Registered Nurse, and she spoke with intellect and compassion.

So, I sat with my thoughts for a few weeks, weighing out all the possibilities. I spoke with people I trusted about my concerns, my hopes, and my fears. I weighed out every single possibility, including my own self-reflection, and debated whether I was "ready" for this.

I thought to myself to stop being silly, that of course I was for this, so stop wasting time. I went online, opened the link, and then ordered the kit. I then sent a message to my biological dad's sister, "I ordered the kit. You will see my results in a few weeks after I receive it and send in my sample."

What happens next is anything short of destiny, perfect timing, and divine intervention once again. God knew exactly when the right time would come to answer my unresolved questions and fulfill my prayers. It was a blessing to realize that HE had been listening all along and waiting for me to take action.

A great surprise was in store for me.

(Look for Book # 3 to conclude)

MY FATHER; ON ANGELS WINGS

Have you ever witnessed a shooting star
Fall brightly from the sky

Then, as suddenly as it caught your eyes
It quickly fades

I imagined who I could have been
If only you have stayed

I'll never understand why
You couldn't stick around
Instead, I compared each man to you
As each one let me down

Is this my lot in life and
O' Father, where art thou?

A hired Dad took your place
A substitute- with superficial hugs
And a half-hearted embrace

Did I remind him of you, Father

Each time he looked upon my face?

A resemblance of your reflection
To remind him of my imperfection

A walking half with a missing culture
O' Father, where art thou?

Father, encompassing me is your gift.
I AM MY FATHER'S DAUGHTER

Your voice, I'll never know
I'll never hear, "You are beautiful daughter."
No wise advice on which way to go.

Instead, I'm left with a beating heart
And an imagination of who I thought you'd be

Without a single validation of the Truth about this
The other half of me

So long, Father, I wished we could've met
You remain this absent part of me
I must remind myself to Forget

To be continued…

Made in the USA
Middletown, DE
28 November 2024